BUDAPEST
to BOCA

BUDAPEST *to* BOCA

The Journey from REFUGEE to CORPORATE EXECUTIVE to ENTREPRENEUR

TOM HERSKOVITS

BUDAPEST to BOCA

The Journey from Refugee to Corporate Executive to Entrepreneur
By Tom Herskovits

First Edition
Copyright © 2026 by Tom Herskovits

Published by
Munn Avenue Press
300 Main Street, Ste 21
Madison, NJ 07940
MunnAvenuePress.com

For permission requests, contact MunnAvenuePress.com

Paperback ISBN: 978-1-969679-25-4
Hardcover ISBN: 978-1-969679-26-1

Printed in the United States of America

CONTENTS

JOURNEY OF AN ENTREPRENEUR

APPENDIX

PREFACE

My journey from Budapest to Boca is more than a change of geography—it is a testament to the complicated path that led from the turmoil of postwar Hungary to the peaceful view from my window in sunny Boca Raton, Florida, as pictured on the cover. Remembrance is a central focus of this memoir, and my recollections focus on the fact that while my life was initially shaped by extreme hardship, I ultimately experienced many periods of joy and satisfaction.

The chronicle of events and learnings is also an expression of gratitude. This book is dedicated to family, friends, and mentors who stood by me and guided and encouraged me to succeed.

I am especially grateful to Dr. Michael Lewis, whose magnificent book *Getting Wiser* inspired me to reflect more deeply on my own story. His encouragement and the opportunity to share my story of overcoming adversity in his book helped spark the idea for this memoir. I also wish to thank those who contributed to my mother's book, *Once a Flower, Always a Flower,* which honored her survival during the Holocaust and set me up to share more about our family's journey in the years that followed.

In the Appendix, a list of lessons learned is provided. They capture insights and principles that have guided me. I am hopeful that, given my challenging childhood and the somewhat unconventional journey through both the structured corridors of major corporations and the often unpredictable terrain of entrepreneurship, I can offer some perspective that may help those navigating these paths.

As my story unfolds, key figures who have shaped my journey are highlighted in grey boxes. Each offers a brief portrait or anecdote, celebrating the unique ways these individuals influenced my path.

The Appendix also includes my final thoughts, which express my appreciation for the life made possible by our great country and my confidence in our future. While I am not an expert on our complex societal issues, I do comment on the challenges we face and the approaches that I believe will be necessary to address them.

Finally, the Appendix contains a list of people I have encountered throughout my life travels.

MEMORIAL

THIS BOOK IS DEDICATED TO DAVID MICHAEL HERSKOVITS, my beloved son, who we lost to an unexpected heart attack at age thirty-eight. His passion for life and commitment to making the world better inspire me every day.

The memorial included here is a small tribute to his profound impact.

* * *

September 7, 1950, Rajka, Hungary—Near the Austrian Border

This was not how it was supposed to happen.

After miles of trudging through mud-ridden fields, we should have been safely across the Austrian border. Instead, Russian troops surrounded us, their guns drawn. My mother, Terry, stood frozen, tears streaming down her face. She heard gunfire, the screams of horror, and then silence. She could only assume that her beloved husband Andy had been killed. My sister, Judy, only one and a half years old, and I, just three and a half, were terrified, huddled in knee-high mud. We held onto each other, not knowing what was happening.

A burly Russian soldier approached Terry and, in broken Hungarian, growled, *"Ha megfordulsz és odamész a gyerekekhez, lelőlek és megölöm őket,"* or *"If you turn around and go to the children, I will shoot you and kill them."* She was dragged away, leaving her children behind, her cries piercing the cold night air.

Terry eventually ended up in the notorious no-visitor prison reserved for those who tried to escape. She would not see her children or know their whereabouts for the next two years. Although she never actually saw him, she assumed her beloved husband was dead. This was just another chapter in the series of horrific events that shaped her young life. Her incredible story, marked by unyielding courage and determination, ultimately paved the way for the life we enjoy today.

1

MY INCREDIBLE MOTHER

MY MOTHER, TOBA GOLDSTEIN, WAS BORN IN KIVJAZD, Czechoslovakia, on December 13, 1924—the seventh of twelve children in the Goldstein family. Her parents named her Toba, but as she grew older, she changed it to Terry, feeling her original name sounded "too Jewish." That decision was her first act of shaping her own identity in a world that would soon try to erase it.

Terry was her father Asher's favorite. Asher, a master tailor, began work before dawn each day, his hands moving with quiet purpose in the half-light. Terry would rise with him, reading or finishing her homework as he stitched. In those silent mornings, Asher dreamed that his brilliant daughter would become an attorney's assistant, the highest position a young woman could hope for then. Ironically, his granddaughter Judy would one day surpass that dream, becoming a federal judge in the United States.

The Goldsteins were deeply rooted in their Judaism, observing the Sabbath and every holiday with absolute conviction. This faith was not just ritual, it was the bedrock that supported Terry through the darkest chapters of her life. Even as the world around her crumbled, she never abandoned her belief in something greater.

Gizi and Pali Lazar employed my mother, Terry, and then cared for my sister, Judy, while my mother was in jail.

In 1934, the family relocated to Beregszász in search of better opportunities. Instead, they found themselves surrounded by rampant anti-Semitism, a sudden and jarring language shift from Czech to Hungarian, and a scarcity of work. Terry's older sister, Shari, had already moved to Budapest and was captivated by the city's beauty and vibrant life. Longing for more than the daily hardships of Beregszász, Terry joined Shari in Budapest, chasing a vision of possibilities.

At just fourteen, Terry found work with a dress designer named Lazar Gizi. Leaving home at such a young age and carving out a life in a new city revealed the courage and tenacity that would define her future.

World War II and Survival

Between 1939 and 1944, as war engulfed Europe, Terry and Shari remained in Budapest. For a time, Hungarian Jews were shielded from the worst horrors, but that changed in March 1944 when the Nazis occupied Budapest and Adolf Eichmann arrived to oversee the fate of Hungary's Jews. Between May and July of that year, nearly 440,000 Hungarian Jews were deported to Auschwitz.

Sensing the growing danger, Terry and Gizi went into hiding, removing the yellow star they had been forced to wear. A Christian friend and their family risked everything to shelter them in a cramped attic from May until October. They lived in isolation, never daring to leave, each day stretching into the next with suffocating sameness. Terry's hope of safety was shattered when Russian troops discovered her and, instead of liberating her, handed her over to the Germans. Terry was then placed on a transport train filled with young people bound for Auschwitz.[1] Gizi was returned to the ghetto.

---

1 *Once a Flower, Always a Flower* by Terry Goldstein Herskovits with Maryann McLoughlin

As the train rattled away, a Hungarian guard, fixated on Terry, commented on how beautiful she was. In a shocking moment, he grabbed her and threw her from the moving train. As she tumbled down an embankment, she wondered, had she survived months hiding only to die here? Miraculously unhurt, she lay in a stream, shaken but alive. That guard saved her life. None of the others on that train survived.

Lost and disoriented, Terry clung to a single name she remembered: Wallenberg. Raoul Wallenberg, the Swedish diplomat, was rumored to be saving Jews by issuing protective papers and providing refuge in safe houses. Driven by hope and courage, Terry made her way to the Swedish Embassy, forcing herself through a desperate crowd. Wallenberg himself took her in, providing papers that placed her, Gizi, and Gizi's husband, Pali in a Spanish safe house, where they remained until the war's end.

When liberation finally came, Terry surveyed the devastation. Her parents and four of her siblings had perished. Three siblings emigrated to Israel, Shari moved to Brazil, and three others made it to the United States. Her brothers Mickey and Shami fought alongside Moshe Dayan and Ariel Sharon in Israel's War of Independence. Seventeen-year-old Shami was killed in battle, and both he and Mickey are still honored as heroes in Israel.

Raul Wallenberg: Swedish diplomat who saved thousands of Jews, including my mother, Gizi, and Pali, by putting them in safe houses.

Love, Marriage, and a Family's Beginnings

After the war, young men returned from Nazi labor camps, eager to rebuild their shattered lives. Terry had many suitors, but when her cousin Shimi introduced her to Andy Davidovits, by their second meeting, she was sure he was the one.

Andy was striking, with wavy blond hair, piercing blue eyes, and an athletic build. He was intelligent, charismatic, and a natural leader, credited with orchestrating the escape of hundreds from a Nazi labor camp. A bold entrepreneur, Andy thrived in post-war Budapest, selling contraband cigarettes and providing goods to the Jewish community.

In 1946, Terry and Andy married and moved into a luxurious apartment in Budapest. They dined in the finest restaurants, attended the opera, and dressed in the latest fashions. This life of comfort was a stark contrast to the deprivation they had endured during the war. It was a life Terry never dreamed of.

But even this new life was not without its challenges. Terry became pregnant, looking forward to starting a family. On March 30, 1947, I arrived ten weeks early. I weighed a mere two and a half pounds. The technology used to effectively treat premature infants today was nonexistent at the time. While the doctors gave me virtually no chance to survive, my mother refused to accept the dim prognosis. Her nourishing breast milk brought life into the skinny boy they named Tomas, pronounced Tomash.

By four months old, I was not only surviving but thriving. The doctors called it a miracle. My continued growth and the birth of my sister, Judy, in April 1949, brought great joy to the Davidovits family.

Unlike my difficult beginning, Judy was the perfect baby: rosy cheeks, beautiful hair, and a sweet, vibrant personality. Even as a child, she charmed everyone with her radiant smile—an ability she has maintained to this day.

The Decision to Escape—A Betrayal

While we enjoyed our life of luxury in Budapest, the world around us was undergoing rapid change. In 1949, Hungary became the People's Republic of Hungary, a Soviet puppet state under the ruthless dictator Joseph Stalin. I remember having to kiss a bust of Stalin every day before entering school. The Communists nationalized industry and agriculture and dropped an "Iron Curtain" across Hungary and its neighbors. Private enterprise was suppressed, and human rights were all but extinguished. Every aspect of life, including commerce, was controlled by the state. Doing business for personal profit was strictly forbidden.

The Communist repression was enforced by secret police who routinely broke into homes on unconfirmed rumors of disloyalty and arrested the occupants. Also affected by the rigid Communist control was the opportunity to practice religion. Most Jewish institutions were shuttered, and Jewish activists were jailed. Immigration to Israel was not allowed. Anti-Semitism was rampant.

It soon became clear that our family's way of life could not survive. Andy was under investigation for his entrepreneurial activities, and my parents realized we were in grave danger. They decided we had to escape.

Andy meticulously planned every detail. He mapped out the route to the border and arranged for a guide to lead us across the final stretch into Austria. Transportation in Austria was waiting to whisk us to Vienna, where we were to meet up with my godparents and my father's best friend, Erno Fleisher, and his family.

But something went terribly wrong.

Years later, Terry discovered the truth. The guide hired to lead us to safety betrayed us. Because of Andy's stature, he was a valuable target. The guide sold us out to the Russians, giving them precise details about our escape plan and leading us straight into a trap. This act of greed and betrayal had disastrous consequences.

2

POST-DISASTER

THE EVENTS OF THE NEXT FEW WEEKS FOLLOWING THE border disaster are hazy. No one was in a position to fully understand what happened. We do know that Terry was thrown in jail, tried without legal representation, and sentenced to four years in prison. Judy and I were taken somewhere together. The media in Austria reported on the border incident, and Gizi identified our location. She swooped in, probably bribed the Russians, and took Judy. She concluded she could not manage two children, and I was left behind.

From this point on, my memories become clearer. I vividly recall being transported in the back of a truck to a location about half an hour outside of Budapest. It was an orphanage housed in an old barn. There were bunks lined up along the walls, a small kitchen, and a single toilet located just outside the building. There was a murky lake nearby, which I soon learned was the source of most of our food. The two dozen or so children living there survived on the slimy, filthy fish caught from that pond. My aversion to seafood, even to this day, stems from that awful experience.

Each morning began with a run around the lake, followed by menial chores like peeling potatoes. Lunch was a nauseating fish stew that I avoided. In the afternoons, we cleaned the facility and played a few games, followed by dinner. I still remember the strange joy I felt when the potatoes I had peeled showed up on my plate—it was the only edible part of the meal. At night, I shared a lumpy twin bed with an older, much larger boy. Sleep was rare. I mostly lay awake wondering what would happen to me.

Although it felt like an eternity, a few months later, just before Christmas, the stern woman who supervised us told me to pack my meager belongings. My heart pounded with a mix of fear and hope as I stepped outside. To my great joy and relief, I saw a familiar face—a woman from Szombathely. I was ecstatic when I found out she was picking me up to take me there.

Szombathely is a charming village near the Austrian border where my godparents and Erno Fleischer and his family lived. We had visited there often and enjoyed the relief from the crowds and commotion of Budapest.

When we arrived by train, we were met at the Szombathely station by my godmother's sister, Kato, her husband, Béla, and other friends. The warmth of their welcome was overwhelming after the cold isolation of the orphanage.

I moved in with Kato and Béla, whose apartment overlooked a forest preserve and even had a balcony. I had my own room, an unimaginable luxury.

Kato was gentle and nurturing, a woman who did not have children of her own. Béla, her husband, was brilliant and highly respected, not just in Szombathely but across Hungary. He was an internationally ranked chess player, and in Hungary, chess was a national passion, second only to soccer and perhaps water polo.

At first, Béla resisted my presence. He was a structured individual who did not want his routines disrupted. Kato, who did not win many family arguments, prevailed. She had cared for me during previous visits and was convinced that I would enhance their lives.

Once a new routine was established, Béla's reluctance turned to enthusiasm, and we quickly developed a warm relationship. Within weeks, he was treating me like a son. Over time, he presented me as his son to the outside world.

Béla and Kato—a chess champion and his sweet wife, who provided a loving home in Szombathely while the Russians jailed my mother.

To Béla's surprise, even at four years old, I already knew how to play chess thanks to Pali, who had taught me the basics and, to his frustration, had endured me beating him occasionally.

Béla was another story. He began teaching me the intricacies of the game, including the movement of pieces, offense, defense, move projections, and other key concepts essential to winning. We played every day—from the moment I returned from school until late in the evening. He never once let me win. A draw felt like a major victory. Whenever I lost, Béla would carefully reset the board exactly as it had been and show me where I went wrong. His memory and knowledge of chess were extraordinary. Under his guidance, I became a strong player.

Chess became more than a game; it was a way for Béla to teach me patience, strategy, and resilience. Béla also taught me religion, reinforcing the things my parents had taught me about Judaism. He was a "closet Jew." The government subsidized his chess career, and he was forced to be a Communist. They did not tolerate any religion, particularly Judaism. Béla learned and taught in secret. He was extremely knowledgeable about all aspects of Judaism, and he laced his chess instruction with religious teachings. Each lesson, whether chess or religion, was a reminder that even in a world turned upside down, there were things of value that I could learn and master.

In December 2025, we saw the play *Chess* on Broadway. It was almost biographical and reinforced the importance of chess in Russia and Eastern European countries. It made me recognize that even at my young age, I was close to being engulfed in the world of chess, much the way that Béla was in his youth.

In addition to chess, I was doing well in school, scoring high on the battery of tests given to children entering elementary school. Before I turned six, I was identified as a potential future architect, a prestigious and highly respected profession in Hungary.

Due to my academic and chess skills, I was grouped with two other children at school who had similar profiles. We received special instruction in algebra and geometry as early as second grade and spent our afternoons getting schooled in and playing chess.

Having three standout players from such a small town was rare. It was a competitive environment, with all three of us striving to make Hungary's under-twelve chess team. Although I was younger than the others, I had the advantage of learning from one of the world's best players. Unfortunately, as the Russian domination of Hungarian life grew, they disbanded all the Hungarian chess teams.

Looking back, I realize how profoundly Kato and Béla shaped my life. I believed that both my parents were dead, discounting what I was told, that my mother was very sick and in a hospital. Béla and Kato provided the support I desperately needed to face the future. Their home was a place where I learned to believe in myself and to face the challenges ahead with confidence. While others around me at the intermission of *Chess* wondered why tears filled my eyes, Rita and my sister Judy recognized that the memories of Szombathely and the wonderful couple who had cared for me were deeply emotional.

A Hospital or a Jail?

In late 1952, my sister Judy and I were taken to visit our mother in prison. I saw Judy a few times a year in Budapest, and we always looked forward to those visits. But this time was different. The confusion and secrecy around what had happened at the border had made me believe that my mother had also died. While I was told she was very sick and in a hospital, I never believed it. Yet here she was, very much alive, not in a hospital, but a prison.

I wanted to understand what crime my mother could have committed, but no one would give me a clear answer. For Judy and me, that visit was emotional and bewildering. But in retrospect, it is hard to imagine the pain my mother must have felt. She had not seen her children in over two years. She was terrified that we would not recognize or accept her, especially given her gaunt, unkempt appearance. While Judy and I did not know all the events of the past, we not only accepted her but also felt the love that children have for their mothers under normal conditions. We also shared the pain and anguish that was on her face and in her trembling voice.

3

OUT OF JAIL

TERRY WAS RELEASED FROM PRISON IN MAY 1953. MY EMOTIONS were tangled and conflicted. I was relieved to know my mother was alive, but I dreaded leaving the comfort and stability of life in Szombathely for the uncertainty that awaited me in Budapest. I stayed to conclude the school year and continued with my chess commitments. Meanwhile, Judy and my mother moved in with Gizi and Pali. I joined them in mid-summer, and it quickly became clear that this living arrangement could not last.

I never liked Pali, and I doubt he liked me. He was a serious chess player, and perhaps he resented a six-year-old beating him virtually every time. One day, as I yelled out "checkmate," Pali hit me. My mother saw it. That moment made her realize that she needed to find a partner, someone who could be a father to her children and provide a stable home for them.

A friend introduced her to Nathan Herskovits. At their very first meeting, she decided she would marry him. She was twenty-nine, still stunning despite all she had endured, and Nathan was instantly smitten. It seemed unlikely that an eligible bachelor would be interested in a woman with two children. Still, after meeting Judy and me, Nathan confided to his friend that we made him even more certain about Terry.

When she asked me if she should marry him, I answered with the honesty of a somewhat gifted and practical child: "If he can support us, marry him." And she did, just six weeks later, on March 30, 1954, my seventh birthday.

Nathan was a handsome young man with light brown hair and sparkling blue eyes. Like so many Hungarian Jews, he had survived years in a German labor camp. He had been married and had a son. In 1948, just days before his son was born, he escaped Communist Hungary for Israel. He fought in the 1948 Israeli War of Independence, returned home, divorced, and took custody of his two-year-old son, also named Tommy.

A New Family Formed

Life in Hungary in the mid-1950s was dire. Food was scarce. Housing was worse. The three of us—my mother, Judy, and I—moved in with Nathan and his son into a single, cramped room. The entire living space was about fifteen by twelve feet. There was a tiny kitchen and a bathroom that we shared with an elderly woman. Judy, our new stepbrother Tommy, and I shared a double bed, with Judy in the middle and the two Toms on either end, our feet pointing in opposite directions. Judy's feet were constantly tickled, especially when we woke in the middle of the night to the sounds of our apartment mate relieving herself in her bili pot. Nathan and my mom slept in the other twin bed. It was quite a way to begin a marriage.

Nathan and I barely spoke. Tommy and I did not get along. He was hyperactive, while I was serious and reserved. Our personalities and interests just did not mesh. My days of elite chess training were over. While chess was a highly valued activity in Russia, by the time I arrived in Budapest, it had been banned along with all other extracurricular activities. It seemed they also put significant limitations on education. I sat in a crowded classroom with a teacher whose only purpose seemed to be keeping the kids in check.

Thankfully, due to my designation as a future architect, I had two advanced courses: structural engineering and calculus. It was challenging for a fourth grader, but those classes were far more interesting than the rest of the curriculum. During this time, I often traveled to Szombathely, and Judy stayed with Gizi—necessary breaks for both of us.

The Revolution Begins

In 1956, Hungary erupted. Imre Nagy's promise of independence electrified Budapest. Protests began in October, led by university students demanding more political freedom, an end to Soviet oppression, and the removal of Russian troops from Hungary.

I recall a moment, decades later, in 1999, when I sat with friends at a theater in Wilmette, Illinois. The movie *Sonnenschein* featured a newsreel: a trolley arriving in Budapest's central square, with students gathering and the crowd stopping the trolley, forcing the people inside to get out and walk. I stared at the screen in disbelief. I was on that trolley, coming home from school, a frightened nine-year-old who did not fully understand what was happening and what he was supposed to do. I made my way through the square, not knowing that I was part of history.

The revolution was brutal for the Hungarian freedom fighters. Once the Soviets recognized the magnitude of the outbreak, the response was swift and merciless: 2,000 tanks and over 100,000 troops poured into the streets of Budapest to crush the rebellion. They pulled in soldiers from all over the country, even from the borders, to fight the demonstrators.[2]

With the borders less guarded, a narrow window of opportunity opened for people to escape to Austria. Nathan, with his resourcefulness and connections, had access to trucks and knew how to deal with Russian guards at checkpoints—vodka was a more effective currency than money. He helped over a hundred people escape.

Terry was traveling, returning from her childhood home, now part of Ukraine. Nathan agonized over whether he could ask Terry to risk another escape, haunted by the repercussions of Terry's earlier attempt.

---

2 *Once a Flower, Always a Flower* by Terry Goldstein Herskovits with Maryann McLoughlin

The remarkable thing was how certain she was that we had to go. She had just come home on the train and cowered in the corner as anti-Semites were yelling that Hitler should have killed all the Jews. She wanted a better life for her kids. Terry just found out that she was pregnant, and she knew escape would be difficult. Nevertheless, she declared:

We need to go, and we need to go now!

I was apprehensive, but excited about the promise of this faraway idyllic land. Béla had led me to believe that America was the land of limitless opportunities. He would often tell me how much Andy, my biological father, wanted Judy and me to grow up in a free land where our talents would be recognized and rewarded. He gave his life trying to achieve that goal. His sentiments have remained a strong motivating force in my life.

Judy was supportive, particularly given my mother's strong declarations. Tommy decided to stay in Hungary with his mother.

A Successful Escape

On December 7, 1956, we packed our meager possessions into a couple of suitcases and set out for the border. We traveled in one of Nathan's big trucks, crammed with sixteen adults and two children. Nathan drove; Terry sat in the passenger seat holding Judy. At each checkpoint, Nathan handed the Russian guards bottles of vodka, and they waved us through.

Several miles from the border, we left the truck and began to walk. All night we trudged through wasteland, mud sucking at our shoes, as the hills and soggy fields stretched endlessly before us. Whenever the Russians fired light rockets overhead, we dropped into the mud, hearts pounding. The whole ordeal echoed our disastrous attempt in 1950, the fear and uncertainty pressing in with every step.

Nathan, remarkably strong, carried a suitcase in each hand and Judy on his shoulders. I struggled with two suitcases, one filled with my flannel shirts, the other with a collection of every known Russian and Hungarian stamp and coin, a treasure given to me by Béla. That collection would be worth a fortune today, but in my exhaustion and confusion, I dropped the coins and stamps and carried only the shirts across the border.

During one precarious moment, tragedy nearly struck again. As the Russian light rockets soared overhead, my mother and I got separated from the rest of the group. She wanted to turn right, but I felt sure we should go the other way. Despite my notorious lack of direction, for once, I was right.

When we finally reached the border, we collapsed in the mud, utterly spent. I fell asleep where I landed, too tired to care about anything but rest. Nathan, ever the rescuer, walked several more miles on his own and returned with trucks that took us to a nearby Austrian village. There, we were given food and a chance to clean up. From the town, we traveled to Vienna.

We had made it. We had crossed the border to freedom. Estimates are that roughly 200,000 Hungarians successfully fled the country. While the United States accepted over 40,000 Hungarians, strict quotas for Jews were already exceeded by the time we applied. Legislation to increase the Jewish quota never passed, but we had persuasive relatives with cash who were working on our behalf.

4

ON THE *US GENERAL WALKER*

ARRIVING IN VIENNA FELT LIKE STEPPING INTO ANOTHER WORLD.
Thanks to the generosity of the many refugees Nathan had helped across
the Hungarian border, we suddenly had resources from gifts pressed into
Nathan's hands by friends who owed him their freedom. For a few dazzling weeks, we lived in luxury. We stayed in a grand hotel, surrounded by
the splendor of Vienna's historic beauty. Every day brought brand new
discoveries: the sweet tang of oranges, the creamy richness of chocolate,
the almost magical taste of bananas—simple delights we had never known
in Hungary. For the first time, I felt a sense of security that let me focus on
possibilities—we had finally escaped the shadow of our past.

But the dream was short-lived. After several weeks, we were transferred to a refugee settlement camp in Salzburg to await documentation.
The contrast was jarring and cruel.

Jewish refugees were crowded into a decrepit army barrack, a world
away from the opulence of our Vienna hotel. On our very first night, a
group of anti-Semitic Hungarian hooligans from neighboring buildings
attacked. It was a bitter irony: these men had also fled Russian tyranny, yet
they clung to their hatred of Jews with a ferocity that survived even exile.

As the thugs gathered outside, Nathan stepped forward, his military experience in Israel suddenly vital. He moved the women and young children to the back of the building and organized a defense. I was no fighter, but I stood behind my stepfather, gripping an iron rod that had once been part of a bed frame, determined to protect my family. The attackers tried to break in, but they were met with a wall of resistance—blunt metal and raw determination. They retreated and never came back.

The weeks that followed were bleak. The squalid conditions: terrible food, unsanitary facilities, and a constant sense of waiting brought back memories of the orphanage. We lived in a limbo of uncertainty, our fate hanging on the decisions of distant officials. Every day, we waited anxiously for news from our relative in America, who was "negotiating" with immigration authorities. If the U.S. turned us away, Australia and Israel would be our next hope.

We were just two days from committing to Australia when the news finally came: Our entry into the United States had been approved. We never learned exactly how this miracle was accomplished, but we were ecstatic. Even now, I sometimes wonder how different our lives might have been as Australians.

Crossing the Atlantic

On February 15, 1957, we boarded an overnight train from Salzburg to a German port. The following morning, we embarked on the *US General Walker*, a military transport ship.[3] The ship, designed for four to five hundred soldiers, now carried over fifteen hundred refugees. It was packed, with long lines for food and few amenities.

The first days at sea were calm. My mother, pregnant and exhausted, managed to rest. Nathan won a few dollars playing cards, and I spent my time on the upper deck, mesmerized by the vastness of the sea and daydreaming about what awaited us in America.

---

3 *Once a Flower, Always a Flower* by Terry Goldstein Herskovits with Maryann McLoughlin

But the peace did not last. On the third day, we hit open water and a relentless storm that battered the ship. My mother became severely ill, and she was confined to the ship's infirmary. There were moments when we feared she might lose the baby.

One evening, Nathan and I made our way to the dining room. What had been a bustling mess hall was now nearly deserted, the storm having left most passengers violently seasick. We sat alone at a long table, eating quietly, the storm howling outside.

As we neared the U.S. coast, the sea finally calmed. Passing the Statue of Liberty and seeing the New York City skyline for the first time was overwhelming. The sunlight dancing between what seemed like endless building shapes and sizes created a dynamic collage of architecture that surpassed anything I ever imagined. It was strong support for my belief that, as a future architect, I was in the right place and in the right profession.

5

SETTLING IN THE USA

Camp Kilmer and U.S. Soil

AFTER DOCKING IN NEW YORK HARBOR, WE WERE TRANSPORTED to Camp Kilmer in New Jersey for processing. It was a military base repurposed for refugee intake, hardly glamorous, but to us, it was sacred ground. We were finally on American soil.

After years of unimaginable obstacles, betrayals, displacement, and survival, we had arrived. We stood at the threshold of a new life, in the land of freedom and opportunity—ready, at last, to begin the next chapter of our journey.

A Home in Brooklyn

At Camp Kilmer, we were met by Terry's brother, Sam, and Nathan's sister, Dorothy. We moved into the Brooklyn apartment of Sam, his wife Hilda, and their two sons, Michael and Jerry. In the first few days, there were emotional reunions with Terry's two other brothers and Nathan's four other siblings.

It soon became clear that two families in a modest three-bedroom apartment would be a tight squeeze. After two weeks, we rented an apartment close by at 311 Lincoln Place. Given the stifling heat, the priority was to purchase an air conditioner with borrowed money from Nathan's sisters. A 15-inch black-and-white TV set was next. The immigrant family with no resources was among the first to have these modern luxuries. Given the language challenge, our TV viewing was limited primarily to wrestling. Haystacks Calhoun and Killer Kowalsky, famous 1950s wrestlers, became our first American heroes.

The two things that needed immediate attention were a job for my stepfather, Nathan, and school for Judy and me.

Nathan was thirty-seven, had limited formal education, and spoke no English. Complicating things further, the U.S. was in a recession, with unemployment above 7 percent. His experience supervising transportation in Hungary had little value in New York. But with four, soon to be five mouths to feed, Nathan was willing to take on anything. At one point, he had three jobs: moving furniture, loading Coke bottles, and working in a bakery; 18 hours of backbreaking work. But he was clever and soon improved his outlook.

Entering American Schools

The transition to American schools went smoothly for Judy. She learned English quickly and entered the local public school in the second grade. It was here that she began the next sixteen years of academic excellence.

My experience was more complicated.

The public schools would not accept a non-English-speaking fifth grader. I was sent to an Orthodox Yeshiva on Eastern Parkway with my cousins, Michael and Jerry. On my first day, my cousins neglected to meet me after class. I was left to find my way home on the subway. For the next four hours, I wandered the complex New York City transit system, trying to find Underhill Avenue. I kept saying "Uunnderrhill, Uunnderrhill," but no one understood and most avoided the strange little boy trying to find the way home. Finally, a transit cop took pity on the boy and listened carefully. Underhill Avenue was identified, and the path home was defined.

When I finally emerged from the Underhill Avenue train station at around 9 p.m., my mother was there to greet me. The emotional reunion with my mom felt oddly similar to our near-separation at the Hungarian border, though this time, my poor sense of direction was the culprit.

There were academic hurdles, too. Because I did not speak English or Hebrew, I was placed in the first grade. It was comical. I was tall and gangly, about two feet taller than my classmates, with a crew cut and no payes (long sideburns). While the others learned basic addition, I sat there with calculus and structural engineering still fresh in my mind.

In this new world, another guiding figure emerged: Rabbi Moshe Moskowitz, my Hebrew teacher. After class, he pulled me aside and offered me some solid advice: *"Let the Hebrew go in one ear and out the other. Learning English quickly will be the key to your success."* He tutored me during recess and after class, giving me the tools and encouragement I needed. I took his advice to heart. I stopped speaking Hungarian, insisting my parents speak only English. I watched television, mimicked the sounds, and looked up every unfamiliar word. That battered dictionary became my bible.

Our family picked up English faster than most Hungarian refugees. By fall, thanks to Rabbi Moskowitz's advocacy and my growing language capability, I skipped from the first to the fifth grade. This rather unprecedented move was successful due to my solid background in math and science, and Rabbi Moskowitz, who overlooked my weakness in Hebrew.

As school started, my brother Mark was born on September 24, 1957. He made his presence known with loud, persistent wails. While Judy and I were at times disturbed, Mark was cute, and over time, we grew to love having "the Kid" around. Even now, as a grandfather, Mark is still "the Kid," and we still love having him around.

Rabbi Moskowitz was a Hebrew teacher and English tutor, responsible for my academic progress.

Focus on Hoops

The local playground was a hotbed of basketball. Most of the kids were African American, and I quickly became their adopted white kid with a heavy accent and a developing outside shot. I was younger than most, but tall and eager to learn. On weekends, I arrived at sunrise and stayed until dusk, practicing and playing pickup games.

During this period, our family lived parallel lives. Nathan worked tirelessly, and my mother cared for Mark and kept us fed. Judy focused on academics and friendships, and I poured myself into learning English and basketball. My family had no idea how quickly I was improving through playground games, high school, and American Athletic Union leagues, as they never once saw me play.

I also became a baseball fan. Catching a Gill Hodges home run at Ebbets Field made me a Dodgers fan, at least until they deserted Brooklyn.

Judy and I were doing well academically. Our English improved rapidly, and we moved into advanced classes. I even picked up some Hebrew in Rabbi Moskowitz's class. My parents made friends, mostly other Hungarian refugees, and stood out for their improving English.

But one challenge remained: Nathan's job. He was still working at the bakery, laboring in dangerous, overheated conditions for poor pay. Each night, he came home with bloodshot eyes and burned hands. It was clear he needed a change, and we were all ready to support him in finding something better.

6

THE FAMOUS HUNGARIAN CHEF

NATHAN ATTACKED THE CLASSIFIED ADS LIKE A MAN ON A mission. Every morning, he pored over the listings at the kitchen table, circling possibilities and muttering to himself. Day after day, he studied every opportunity until a pattern emerged—there was a demand for chefs. One morning, he looked up from the paper, eyes shining with determination, and announced to the family: *"I'm going to be a famous Hungarian chef."*

We laughed. The idea seemed almost absurd. Nathan could make a few Hungarian dishes, but to call him a competent cook, let alone a famous one, was a real stretch. Still, he was absolutely serious.

As expected, his new career got off to a rocky start. The first three restaurants that hired him quickly realized he wasn't quite ready for prime time, and each let him go. Some might have given up, but not Nathan. Each setback only fueled his resolve. He watched, he listened, he learned. My mother taught him treasured family recipes. His sisters, particularly Dorothy, the oldest, pitched in, sharing their kitchen tricks and secrets that had been passed down through generations. Nathan absorbed it all, practicing late into the night, determined to master his craft. Within a few months, he transformed himself into a skilled cook, worthy of the title of famous Hungarian chef.

Moving to New Jersey

His newfound skills were evident when Nathan interviewed at the Village Delicatessen and Restaurant in Clifton, New Jersey. He could now make flavorful stews, schnitzel, potato pancakes, and knishes with ease. He was confident and ready for a new challenge. He got the job.

The deli was both a restaurant and a bustling takeout counter, and Nathan quickly adapted to both roles. He handled the lunch rush, filled catering orders, and built strong relationships with customers. The regulars came to know him, not just as a chef, but as a friend. For the first time in America, Nathan found joy and pride in his work.

But there was one problem: the commute.

Each day, Nathan traveled an hour and a half each way from Brooklyn to Clifton—three hours on buses and subways, six days a week. He was exhausted. By the summer of 1959, we knew something had to change.

We rented a house in Clifton, just blocks from the delicatessen. It was a significant step up from our cramped Brooklyn apartment as it had three spacious bedrooms, modern features, and, for the first time, a car. That car gave us a new sense of freedom and possibility as a family.

For me, the biggest perk was just a half-block away: a basketball court. The court belonged to the local elementary school. Compared to the fierce competition of Brooklyn, the suburban games were a breeze. I was the tallest player there, and the experience on the city's rough courts gave me an undeniable edge.

As my bar mitzvah approached, my parents enrolled me at Hillel Academy to continue my Hebrew education. I was finally placed in the right grade level, and I excelled academically.

However, one week before my bar mitzvah, I faced the only time in my life I contemplated suicide. I was starting my practice session with the rabbi when he shouted, *"That is the wrong portion."* The scripture portion I studied for nine months was not the right one. For the kid who let Hebrew in one ear and out the other, learning a new lengthy portion in one week seemed impossible. For the next six days, I skipped school and listened to a recording of the correct portion and memorized it. I still view the fact that I was able to perform without mistakes in front of over two hundred people as the biggest challenge I have ever overcome.

A Family Name

While life in Clifton was a significant improvement, beneath the surface, one issue simmered: my last name.

Nathan felt strongly that Judy and I should be formally adopted and change our last name from Davidovits to Herskovits. He was proud of us and wanted the world to see Judy and me as his own children. But I still felt a deep obligation to my biological father and wanted to honor him by keeping the Davidovits name. I resisted the change, clinging to the last thread of my old identity.

In hindsight, I realize I was wrong. Nathan had overcome enormous challenges. He had worked himself to the bone, built a new life for all of us, and given us stability and love. He deserved to have the children he raised carry his name. Ultimately, it was my mother who convinced me. For the good of the family, I agreed to the change. In August 1961, Judy and I were formally adopted and changed our last name to Herskovits.

7

SETTLING IN CLIFTON

THINGS CONTINUED TO MOVE IN A POSITIVE DIRECTION FOR the Herskovits family. Nathan became a partner in the Village Delicatessen, and under his steady leadership, the business thrived. We bought an attractive house in Clifton, with a stunning view of the New York City skyline, a daily reminder of how far we had come. I joined Judy in the local public school system, and Mark started nursery school.

Judy and I continued to do well academically, consistently ranking near the top of our classes. I remained focused on becoming an architect, while Judy excelled in every subject she tackled. The teacher who left the greatest mark on my high school years was Miss Donatelli, my German teacher for four years. She not only taught me German but also tutored me in English, further refining my language skills. Thanks to her guidance, I improved on the English section of the SATs, complementing my perfect Math score.

My two best high school friends also deserve mention. Doug Ivan, my basketball teammate, was voted most likely to succeed in our class. He went on to a successful career as a physician. Ken Goren, who lived in my neighborhood, became my close friend, college roommate, and later my companion in the army. Ken and his brother would eventually build their father's hardware business into a successful chain.

While Judy and I were busy with academics, sports, and other activities, we also both worked in the deli. Judy managed the cash register. I was the grill man and

> *CLIFTON HIGH*
> *Ms. Donatelli —German teacher and English tutor; Doug Ivan— good friend; successful physician. Ken Goren, a good friend, built a solid hardware business*

served customers at the counter. The grill was in the front window, so I was pretty much on display for all spectators to see. I flipped burgers, steaks, and hot dogs, juggling as many as a dozen orders at once.

At the counter, I became known for my ability to cut smoked salmon. I had my own knife, which I kept extremely sharp, allowing me to produce uniform and paper-thin slices. I was also instrumental in developing a frozen entrée line featuring delicious soups and meals such as Salisbury Steak, Chicken Fricassee, Veal Milanese, and other sumptuous dishes. Although more expensive than competing products, it was food that you were proud to serve. This was my first entrepreneurial venture.

Business started slowly, but once customers tried our meals, demand surged. Some would buy over $100 worth at a time. One of our regulars was the frozen food buyer at ShopRite. I convinced him to test our line in one of their stores, and despite minimal marketing, it was a hit. Our product expanded to five ShopRite locations. Unfortunately, further expansion required USDA inspection at our facility. My father didn't want that added layer of regulation, so we scaled back, eventually serving just one store. That decision cost us our placement and an exciting opportunity.

Another idea I was enthusiastic about: bagels. At the time, bagels were a niche product, but I sensed they were destined for broader success. The bakery next door to our deli made excellent bagels, and I lobbied my father to buy the business. Before Lender's Bagels became a household name, I had tested frozen bagels and found they came out of the oven just as delicious as fresh bagels. I was confident I could sell them to my contact at ShopRite. My father was impressed, but ultimately uninterested in running a bakery. Years later, while working at Kraft, I was involved in the acquisition of Lender's Bagels. After the deal closed, I sent my father a copy of the sizable check we gave the Lender brothers, along with a note: "This could have been yours." The bagel category exploded, growing from a modest $300,000 industry to over $7 billion today.

Though my big ideas weren't fully realized at the time, I was paid for my work at the deli, and in the summer of 1961, I earned my lifeguard certification and worked at The Pines Hotel in the Catskills. I also bused high-stakes poker games in the evenings, and the tips were outstanding.

The next summer, I added another job to my résumé: selling *Encyclopedia Britannica*. I sold a record twenty-eight sets, which brought the national sales manager to see me in action. Instead of following the EB script, I created my own approach, selling parents of college-bound students the SAT prep program that came bundled with the encyclopedias. My personal certificate for a perfect 800 Math score was a valuable prop unless the customer asked about my English score, which was 520 on the first test, eventually raised to 690 working with Miss Donatelli. After my first presentation, the manager gave me a stern reprimand, but after seeing a few more successful sales calls, he relented, and soon, my pitch was integrated into the Britannica presentation.

About six months before my seventeenth birthday, the legal driving age in New Jersey, I had saved the $3,350 I needed to buy my own car: a 1964 maroon Pontiac Le Mans. It was almost identical to my dream car, the GTO, but at a much lower price. I loved that car and drove it for over 200,000 miles.

My three years at Clifton High flew by. I did well in school and had an active social life. I played basketball in leagues filled with ex-college players. The summer before my senior year, I played at Kushner's in the Catskills and held my own against college athletes. I built connections with several coaches. I felt confident I could become a world-class architect and a solid college basketball player.

While I was focused on my academic and athletic future, the United States and the world were in turmoil. Thirteen days in October 1962 brought humanity close to nuclear war. U-2 photos of Soviet missiles in Cuba forced President Kennedy to impose a naval quarantine. A secret deal with Khrushchev avoided disaster. I can recall trying to convince a young lady in my German class that, with nuclear war on the horizon, this may be her last chance to ... never mind, the approach did not work.

A year and a month later, in the same German class, a disturbing message came over the intercom: ***"President John F. Kennedy has been shot and killed in Dallas, Texas."*** No one said a word. We just sat in disbelief.

The chaos continued in 1964, when we began our long and painful involvement in Vietnam. By 1969, over 500,000 US troops were fighting a war that was not supported by a majority of the country. By the war's end, almost 60,000 Americans and 3 million Vietnamese and Cambodians had died.

Despite it all, my family remained focused and somewhat distant from each other. Neither my parents nor siblings ever came to a basketball game or engaged with my or Judy's academic or social life. The deli was the priority for all. Our lives were built on hard work, and our steady climb reflected the determination of immigrants building a future in America.

8

PICKING A COLLEGE

THROUGHOUT HIGH SCHOOL, MY PRIORITIES NEVER WAVERED: I wanted to study architecture at a top program and play major college basketball.

The Ivy League offered several excellent architecture schools, and the University of Pennsylvania stood out. Its faculty included the legendary Louis Kahn, along with other highly respected architects. The basketball coach, Jack McCluskey, had a solid reputation, and the school was just a short ride from Clifton. But like all Ivy League schools, Penn did not offer athletic scholarships.

Of all the other schools I considered, Syracuse University rose to the top. Its School of Architecture was highly rated, and its basketball program was on the rise, becoming a national powerhouse. I narrowed my choices to Penn and Syracuse, and scheduled campus visits.

My first visit was to Penn. I was especially excited about the possibility of meeting Louis Kahn, a primary reason I was drawn to the school. I was told he didn't meet with prospective students. But thanks to some encouragement from Coach McCluskey, I was granted a brief, fifteen-minute meeting.

It did not go well.

I struggled to relate to the abstract nature of what Kahn discussed. While he was one of the great architects of the 20th century, he had trouble communicating clearly, or perhaps I was in a state of awe in the presence of such a renowned architectural master. There was also no time for questions or any further discussion. Frankly, I was happy to leave his office. An hour later, I was still attempting to decipher our conversation.

As I transitioned from the architecture building to the gym, I had a chance to visit with a couple of architecture students and was struck by their lack of enthusiasm for the school. While I was impressed by Coach McCluskey, the overall experience left me cold. The visit was brief and ultimately disappointing.

Two weeks later, I flew to Syracuse on a Thursday morning. A junior basketball player picked me up at the airport and drove me straight to Manley Field House, a brand-new, state-of-the-art facility. It seated nearly ten thousand fans, making it one of the largest and most impressive on-campus arenas in the country at the time. As we walked in, I looked up and saw the scoreboard flash: "WELCOME TOM." That small gesture made a big impact. It demonstrated their interest in me.

I met freshman coach Roy Danforth and varsity coach Fred Lewis. They were engaging and welcoming, and I felt like I could be part of something meaningful. I asked for a picture of the scoreboard and the two coaches. They obliged, and a framed picture arrived at my place the next day.

I spent most of the following day at Slocum Hall, home to the School of Architecture. My host was Professor Emeritus Lou Skoler, a talented architect and outstanding educator. His designs were impressive, and I found his vision for the school's future inspiring. We discussed the past and future of architecture at length. I was also impressed by the student work displayed in a line of beautiful, well-presented cabinets with innovative designs. These "reserves" were displayed for five years. That night, I attended a fraternity party, which added to my positive experience.

It was an easy decision. Despite the appeal of an Ivy League school, Syracuse would be my college home.

After graduating from Clifton High, I had a relatively quiet summer. I worked full-time at the deli and played a lot of basketball. Initially, I expected to take out student loans to cover the cost of college. But then Nathan said he would cover my tuition. That act of generosity deepened our relationship. I recognized the full scope of what he had accomplished and the effort and skill that had been required. I also came to understand how deeply he cared for Judy and me. Over time, I not only came to respect him, but I came to love him like a father.

$$9$$

---

285 MILES TO A NEW LIFE

IN EARLY SEPTEMBER 1965, IT WAS TIME TO PACK UP AND HEAD to Syracuse. Freshmen weren't allowed to have cars on campus, but through the grapevine, I learned that enforcement was loose. I brought my beloved Pontiac Le Mans with me. The drive from Clifton to Syracuse spanned 285 miles, winding through the Catskills and up Route 81—a route I would take nearly fifty times over the next four years. It was the beginning of a fresh chapter, with many unexpected turns that would shape my future.

When I pulled up to Booth Hall, my dormitory, I was immediately greeted by a warm smile from a beautiful young lady who introduced herself as my "Goon," a sophomore selected to help new students adjust. Goons were chosen based on personality and academic achievement, and being one was a badge of honor. I would become a Goon myself as a sophomore.

My new Goon friend made me feel welcome, helped me settle into the dorm, and showed me around campus. She was an art and design major, so we had a lot to talk about. We had dinner that evening and dated for about the next six months.

The following day, my roommate Kenny Goren arrived. We had grown up a block apart in Clifton and were close friends in high school. But despite sharing a room, we didn't see much of each other that year; our schedules, schools, fraternities, and interests diverged. Years later, we would reconnect unexpectedly as Army basic training bunkmates at Fort Knox.

Architecture and a Painful Rebound

Classes and basketball practice began simultaneously. My schedule was intense: I had an 8:30 a.m. class every weekday and didn't finish until 5:00 p.m. On days with basketball practice, I left early and made up missed classes afterward. The architecture faculty was accommodating, but the workload was relentless. I soon realized why no varsity basketball player had ever enrolled in the School of Architecture.

Basketball practice was also very strenuous—a lot of conditioning work combined with guarding players such as Dave Bing, Jim Boeheim, and fellow freshman Frank Hamlin, who was Mr. Indiana Basketball.

Three weeks into the season, my basketball dream collapsed. I went up for a rebound against Frank, came down on his ankle, and broke mine. I was in a cast for ten weeks, hobbling through snowy campus paths on crutches.

That injury ended my basketball career.

It was devastating but also freeing. I would have struggled to balance the demands of both elite academics and Division I athletics. With sports behind me, I poured all my energy into my studies.

Three of my architectural designs, including fully built models, were graded as reserves. These pieces were displayed in the very same cases I had admired on my first campus tour. Years later, Professor Lou Skoler told me that after five years on display, he had taken one of my models home. That compliment was a highlight of my academic architecture career.

Finger Lakes Retreat and an Inspiring Message

With the relentless pressure of the architecture program, an occasional off-campus jaunt was rejuvenating. The Finger Lakes region was a perfect escape from the academic grind. A series of eleven glacial lakes located about sixty-five miles southwest of Syracuse, it was renowned for its serene natural beauty. It's not a place for fancy hotels, famous golf courses, or five-star restaurants, but only nature's beauty.

Through a good friend, I had access to a magical retreat: a magnificent stone mansion perched on a two-acre island roughly one thousand yards offshore. In the coldest winters, you could walk across the frozen lake to reach it, but most often, we rowed there in the boat docked along the shoreline. The Finger Lakes are exceptionally deep and rarely freeze, even during the bitter Upstate New York winters.

The mansion, called *La Grande*, presumably named for some foreign connection, featured five spacious bedrooms, a grand living and dining area, and a kitchen stocked with frozen food. There was no central heating, but each room had a massive stone fireplace, and stacks of firewood were piled high beside them. The crackling fires not only provided warmth but cast a golden glow that filled the home with a unique and comforting atmosphere.

On my first visit, I drove five friends up for a long weekend. Late that first night, while the others were fast asleep, I sat by the large fireplace in the living room, quietly reflecting.

As I stared into the flames, drifting into a state between consciousness and sleep, I had what can only be described as an out-of-body experience. In the dancing light of the fire, I saw my father—my biological father—as clearly as if he were standing there before me.

I was sure it was him, even though I never saw a picture of him and only knew him until I was three and a half when he was killed at the border. His message was simple—he was very happy that I had made it to America, was proud of all that I had accomplished, and was looking forward to my future.

Andy—My Father

I was still in a daze when I regained full consciousness. Was it a dream? If not, what? I did not tell anyone as it seemed too surreal, too personal, and too complicated to explain.

Years later, Erno, my father's best friend, gave me his picture, and I recognized it as the father who spoke to me that night. Although I barely knew him, he has remained a major source of motivation, as I have always felt he was watching over and supporting me.

10

THE RECORD RUNNER & THE PONIES

After a successful freshman year, I returned to Clifton for the summer. The Village Deli was booming, and Nathan needed help. I worked six days a week.

That summer, my stepbrother, Tommy, from Hungary, visited us. He later immigrated to America in 1978. We had a rocky history, but we were older now, and over time, we actually grew to like each other. I still refer to him as the "real Tom Herskovits."

Eventually, Tommy married Andrea, who also came from Hungary. Tommy and Andrea moved to California, where Tommy built a successful insurance business, and Andrea managed a major department store.

Despite the long hours in the deli, I continued something I had started in high school: maintaining a list of money-making ideas. The frozen bagels and frozen entrées were early entries. Over that summer, the list continued to grow.

One of my early entries expanded on a book we received as freshmen at Syracuse, called the "Pig Book," a simple student directory with photos and basic information. I envisioned a version that provided more detail and eventually evolved into an interactive platform with telephone connections. Years later, when Facebook emerged, I thought: *"I had that idea!*" It joined Béla's stamp and coin collection, which I dropped at the border, as a missed opportunity.

Another idea? Late-night food delivery from the local Marshall Street restaurants to dorms. I abandoned it quickly because the snowy hills, icy roads, and marginal economics didn't add up.

One idea stuck, however.

Record albums were sold to students for $4.50–$5.00, well above the typical retail price of $3.25–$3.50. When I returned in the fall, I found a distributor who sold me records at wholesale prices and delivered them by 5 p.m. the next day. I launched a record-selling operation in my dorm. Sales were modest at first—about fifty albums the first two months—but the foundation was set for something much bigger.

During winter break, I made a bold move: I bought the record distribution company.

The owner, a kind seventy-one-year-old man, was anxious to retire. He accepted my first offer. My roommate helped finance the deal and became a co-owner. We retained the two key employees, making for a smooth transition. This was the initial transaction of my long-term approach to deal-making: thorough research of the acquisition, offering a fair price, and limited or no negotiations.

I named the business "The Record Runner" and expanded the team— five dorm sales reps and one handling fraternity and sorority accounts. Before the school year ended, I placed ads in student newspapers and interviewed and hired campus reps at six other colleges. The groundwork for scaling the business was now in place.

The Record Runner had a breakthrough in the summer of 1967. We purchased five thousand copies of *Sgt. Pepper's Lonely Hearts Club Band* by The Beatles. During the critical first weeks of its release, only the Record Runner had enough inventory to meet the massive demand. We sold out in three weeks, generating a significant profit and, just as importantly, nearly doubling our customer base. I was amazed, given that this happened while most of our campuses were in summer sessions.

Over the next two years, the business continued to grow. We expanded to nine campuses. By my senior year, the Record Runner's profit was more than twice the starting salary of architects.

Glen Garnsey and the Ponies

In addition to the Record Runner, I had another so-called extracurricular activity—harness racing. On Friday nights, a group of guys from my fraternity would go to the local harness track, Vernon Downs. It was a fun evening and a welcome break from academics. At first, I lost money at the races but usually recovered my losses in the poker game that followed. Over time, I got to know the drivers, the trainers, and studied the breeding of the animals. In particular, I started to follow an up-and-coming twenty-two-year-old named Glenn Garnsey. I bet on him almost exclusively and started to win.

Late in my sophomore year, I successfully got the fraternity to claim a horse in a claiming race. On Glen's advice, we claimed a horse named Senga Sway for $4,000, and twenty-two of our brothers watched Senga destroy the field, winning by six lengths. The picture of the brothers in the winner's circle hung in the frat house living room for years to come.

The following week, Senga won again by four lengths. The following week, he had what horsemen call "a tough trip," but Glen still got him second to the finish line. He got claimed for $6,000, and the fraternity's racing days were over. The fraternity's bank account was $4,220 richer, and I found a good friend and partner in the harness business for the next twenty years.

By the time he was thirty years old, Glenn was regarded as the top harness driver in the country. He signed an exclusive contract with Castleton Farms, which allowed him to own up to eight horses in our partnership. We were cash-positive in eighteen of the twenty years we were together. Unfortunately, Glenn died in a car crash at the age of forty-two. I was devastated, and I sold all our horses at prices well below market value.

While getting involved with horse racing was exciting, my focus remained on the Record Runner. In my senior year, I began formulating plans to expand Record Runner nationally. This raised a critical question. Could I become an architect and manage a national business on the side? I did not think so, and neither did my girlfriend, who was about to become my wife.

11

Career, Marriage & the Army

My senior year, 1969, was a turbulent and transformative time, both for me personally and for the country. The Vietnam War raged on, and resistance to U.S. involvement intensified. Massive demonstrations erupted across the nation, including at Syracuse University. That year marked the first televised draft lottery, as the government attempted to make military selection more equitable. I remember contemplating the lottery with a mix of dread and fascination, knowing that a single number could determine my fate.

Richard Nixon was inaugurated as president, promising change in a divided America. In July, the world watched in awe as Neil Armstrong and Buzz Aldrin became the first humans to set foot on the moon, a moment that filled the country with pride and wonder.

On campus, the atmosphere was charged. The use and availability of drugs exploded in colleges across the country, and Syracuse was no exception. Two of my friends died from overdoses, and another was sentenced to a long prison term for drug distribution. I moved out of my fraternity house and into an off-campus apartment to distance myself from the drug scene. As a committed non-user, I found myself increasingly alienated from friends who were heavy users.

Sports in 1969 also made history. The "Miracle Mets" stunned the world by defeating the heavily favored Baltimore Orioles in the World Series. Joe Namath led the New York Jets to a legendary Super Bowl III victory over the NFL's Baltimore Colts. UCLA claimed its third straight NCAA basketball championship, and Boris Spassky dethroned Tigran Petrosian to become World Chess Champion. I followed these events closely, especially the Mets, Jets and Spassky victories, which felt like miracles in a year of upheaval.

For the Record Runner, keeping up with the rapidly changing music industry was essential. 1969 was the year of Woodstock and the rise of artists like Jimi Hendrix, Creedence Clearwater Revival, Sly and the Family Stone, Neil Young, and John Fogerty. The Beatles released *Yellow Submarine* and, later that year, their final album, *Abbey Road*. Our business succeeded in part because we understood the evolving landscape of rock, heavy metal, country, folk-rock, and progressive music.

Decisions, Decisions, Decisions

1969 wasn't just about national milestones; it was a year of major personal decisions. I had to confront the possibility of being drafted, make choices about my career, and perhaps most significantly, commit to marriage. I married Linda Blatt two weeks after graduating in June of 1969.

Linda and I met at the beginning of my junior year when I filled in for a friend as a waiter at the Sigma Delta Tau sorority. It was a house full of beautiful women, but Linda stood out. She had long blonde hair, stunning blue eyes, and a quiet, thoughtful demeanor. She was exceptionally bright, a bridge master, and was studying computers. Linda would go on to become a sought-after expert in the early days of information technology.

We dated throughout my junior year, and during my senior year (her sophomore year), she moved into my apartment. Linda seemed like the perfect life partner: bright, beautiful, Jewish, and my family liked her very much. My sister, Judy, who had a certain veto power in these matters, was particularly enthusiastic.

I was twenty-two and Linda was twenty when we got married. While those ages were typical at the time, in hindsight, neither of us was truly prepared for such a serious commitment.

The Army

Another major decision I faced during senior year was how to avoid being drafted and sent to Vietnam. Despite nationwide protests, the war showed no signs of coming to an end. Many of those drafted never returned. The options were to hope for a high draft number or try to join the reserves.

I decided not to roll the dice on the lottery. The reserves were the choice of many, making it quite challenging to secure a position. I had heard that there were units available in New Jersey with openings. The first three units I visited had no openings. However, to my surprise, when I showed up at a reserve unit in Edison, New Jersey, the woman behind the counter recognized me. She was the mother of a former girlfriend, someone who had always liked me, maybe even more than her daughter. Somehow, I made the list and began my Army career in January 1969.

I received a waiver allowing me to complete college before starting basic training, but I was still required to attend reserve meetings. The unit in Edison was three hundred and fifteen miles from Syracuse, and I had to make that six-hundred and thirty-mile round trip two Wednesdays a month. The drive was brutal, and sitting in a room for three hours was also brutal, but I felt fortunate to have secured the position.

Ironically, my draft lottery number ended up being two hundred and twenty-four out of three hundred and sixty-five—high enough that I most likely would not have been drafted at all.

I was assigned to Fort Knox, Kentucky, for Army basic training in the fall of 1969. Arriving at my barracks, I threw my clothes in my locker and happened to glance at the name of my bunkmate—Ken Goren. Could it be my high school best friend and my Syracuse freshman-year roommate? By an amazing coincidence, yes, it was. After losing touch over the last couple of years at Syracuse, we were back together.

While basic training was rigorous, both Kenny and I were in good shape and actually enjoyed the physical activity. The nightly poker game produced major benefits. Rather than take cash, the losers shined my shoes, made my bed, and cleaned my rifle. Not having these chores made life easier. I returned to Syracuse before the end of 1969, ready to decide the direction of the next chapter.

Architecture or Business

Since the age of six, I had dreamed of becoming an architect. In Hungary, architecture carried status and prestige. My experience at the Syracuse School of Architecture, my relationship with Professor Skoler, and the thrill of creating beautiful, functional designs made the architecture career path hard to abandon.

But the realities were sobering. The Record Runner and my horse partnership had generated more than twice the profits of a starting architect's salary. The business world was full of entrepreneurial opportunities, while new architecture graduates competed for limited openings. The chance to create masterpieces was rare, and it took years to become a lead designer at a major firm. New architects typically handle the drafting of stair, door, and window details for years. Starting a new firm was prohibitively expensive.

By junior year, I had begun taking all my electives in the School of Management, and I enjoyed them. The Record Runner continued to succeed, and the decision became clear. After graduation and basic training, I enrolled in the Syracuse MBA program in early 1970. I was fully committed to my business studies and earned straight A's.

Meanwhile, the Record Runner expanded to four more campuses. The vision was to go national. My wife, Linda, who was then completing her junior year, also earned all A's. We were succeeding academically, though romance had taken a backseat.

As 1971 began, things took an unexpected turn. Two lawyers from a prominent Syracuse law firm visited me. They represented "undisclosed clients" who wanted to buy The Record Runner. They informed me that I was breaking the law by conducting a profit-generating business on university property. The offer was reasonable, so I sold the Record Runner. They then promptly shut it down, confirming my suspicion that their client was the distributor for all the profitable on-campus record stores.

With money in the bank, Linda and I planned to move to Clifton, buy a house, and I would market the Village Deli's soups and entrées to supermarkets. I also considered buying the bakery to sell frozen bagels. My parents were thrilled. Nathan could retire soon and, hopefully, enjoy becoming a grandfather.

But something didn't sit right. While I believed in the Village product line, I was less than enthusiastic about returning to the deli. I couldn't shake the feeling that I wanted to make it on my own.

Dave Wilemon—Mentor and Catalyst

My advisor at Syracuse was my marketing professor, Dr. David Wilemon. Dr. Wilemon was more than a teacher; he was a mentor and friend. He was an imposing figure, about 6'4", a former SMU tackle, and a brilliant marketer.

Together, we were among the first to recommend building an entrepreneurship program at Syracuse. The curriculum was developed in the 1970s and 80s and became one of the nation's

Dr. David Wilemon, a brilliant and personable marketing professor who was my counselor and had a significant positive impact on my life.

top five programs. While many contributed, Dr. Wilemon was a driving force. Years later, I was proud to contribute to this program as a member of the School of Management Advisory Group.

Dr. Wilemon believed I should continue learning in a big company where training and developing young managers was a key priority. Without asking me first, he set up interviews with Bloomingdale's, General Foods, and Procter & Gamble (P&G)—elite training grounds for aspiring executives.

The interviews at Bloomingdale's and General Foods went very well. Both companies had their VPs of Human Resources conduct the interviews, and both made attractive offers within a week.

The P&G interview was conducted a week later by a regional sales manager. It was a half-hour stress interview, full of rapid-fire questions. I then had to take a forty-five-minute aptitude test, and the sales manager indicated that he'd get back to me in a couple of weeks.

Despite Dr. Wilemon's advice, I decided to speak up about what I thought was an inappropriate process. I wrote to Henry Wilson, P&G's VP of HR.

I made three points: First, I stated I wasn't interested in sales. I wanted brand management. I acknowledged that most of their recruits came from Ivy League schools and suggested they were missing out on exceptional candidates by not building relationships with professors and career counselors at schools like Syracuse.

Second, I resented taking the aptitude test, given my academic record. Finally, I correctly pointed out that two questions on the test had no correct answers among the multiple-choice options. I suggested that trying to trick candidates didn't reflect well on a company of P&G's stature. The letter struck the right balance—direct, thoughtful, and a little humorous. I didn't expect a response; I just needed to speak my mind.

A few days later, I was pulled out of class and rushed to the Dean's office. It was an emergency.

The call was from Thomas Laco, Executive Vice President, Procter & Gamble. He introduced himself. We discovered that we shared an immigrant background. He had come to the U.S. from Czechoslovakia at the age of five. He told me he appreciated my letter and thought it might inspire changes in their recruiting process. He thanked me.

I was stunned; this was a top executive at the world's largest consumer goods company, and he was thanking me. He asked me to come to Cincinnati to interview. Dr. Wilemon believed I was the first Syracuse student ever to interview for P&G brand management, one of the most prestigious and selective entry positions in the business world, usually reserved for the brightest at top business schools. Dr. Wilemon was elated. Linda and I were excited, especially since they indicated they would find a suitable job for her. The following week, I headed to Cincinnati.

My visit began with dinner at Maissonette, one of America's finest restaurants, with Assistant Brand Manager Chuck Lieppe. We had a great meal and conversation. It began a friendship that remains to this day. The next day, I interviewed with several brand managers—Lew Ross, Paul Geissler, Ron Gordon, and Jim VanCleave, the promotion manager. They were impressive, engaging, and made the career path clear: in three to four years, I could be running a half-billion-dollar brand.

At the end of the day, Jim VanCleave offered me the position. The offer was highly competitive—and even more attractive considering Cincinnati's low cost of living. Then I was taken to the 11th floor—the executive suite—to meet Tom Laco in person.

It was everything you'd expect: high ceilings, mahogany walls, and thick carpeting. Mr. Laco greeted me like an old friend. We discussed entrepreneurship, brand building, architecture, and our shared experiences. He told me he was confident I would succeed at

Tom Laco—a real gentleman, a great role model, and was very helpful in my transition to the corporate world.

P&G and that I would love it. The next day, I accepted the offer. I would begin my career at Procter & Gamble in Cincinnati, Ohio.

12

GRADUATION AND THE START OF A CAREER

JUNE 5, 1971—GRADUATION DAY AT SYRACUSE UNIVERSITY. I HAD earned a Bachelor of Science degree, double-majoring in architecture and finance, and an MBA. I maintained an excellent academic record, and had every reason to feel proud.

The campus was alive with celebration. Families gathered to honor their graduates, cameras flashed, and laughter filled the air across the quad. But when the name Thomas Herskovits was called, there was no one to walk across the stage, no hand to shake, no cheers from the audience.

Nathan was back in Clifton, working at the deli on one of the busiest days of the year, overwhelmed with catering orders for graduation parties. My mother was at home tending to Mark and Judy. My siblings probably didn't even know graduation was happening. Linda and I were in Cincinnati, as I had already been a week into my career at P&G.

About a month before graduation, I got a call from Paul Geisler, who had interviewed me previously. He told me that if I started on June 1st, I'd likely work on his brand. Paul was the brand manager of Bold detergent, and the chance to work with and learn from him was too good to pass up. I gave up three hours sitting in the sun and a $40 photo of a handshake and diploma for a head start on my career. In hindsight, while I do have the diploma, I sometimes wish I had that picture, too.

Start of a Career at Procter & Gamble

My first day, June 1, 1971, was a scorcher. Temperatures soared into the high eighties. Determined to make a good impression, I arrived early, parking in the garage and stepping into the air-conditioned lobby of P&G headquarters at 6:32 a.m. I pressed the button in the elevator for the ninth floor—the home of the Package Soap and Detergent Division, known as PS&D.

A great beginning at P&G thanks to Paul Geisler and Dean Butler. They were both excellent teachers.

As the elevator doors were closing, a distinguished older gentleman stepped in. I nodded and greeted him. He asked my name. I told him it was my first day.

He replied, *"Hello. I'm Howard Morgens. Why don't you come up to my office for a couple of minutes?"*

My mind raced. The CEO? What should I say next? I managed a nervous, *"Very nice to meet you, sir."*

As the elevator stopped at nine, the door opened and then closed, my mind continued racing–now what? Where would I start? Thankfully, when we got to his office, he started the conversation by asking me where I was born. In the next few minutes, I was able to condense the 13,313 words that I have written so far into about five minutes. He followed with a couple of questions about the Record Runner, architecture, and my expectations of P&G. He made a nice comment about being happy that P&G hired me and wished me good luck. He pressed the button under his desk, and the door opened.

As I left, I thanked his secretary, who seemed startled by my presence. It was probably very unusual for a young person wearing a short-sleeved blue shirt (uniform discussion to follow) to be in Mr. Morgan's office at all, let alone at 7 a.m. I returned to the ninth floor, still in semi-shock.

I hadn't even officially started my job, and I had already met two of the top three executives at the world's largest consumer goods company—and they were kind, engaged, and genuinely interested in my future. Thank you, Dr. Wilemon, for orchestrating this opportunity.

Bold Beginnings

It didn't take long to realize that my Bold assignment was outstanding. Paul Geisler was an experienced and effective brand manager. He and his assistant brand manager (ABM), Dean Butler, were a great team to learn from. Later in his career, Dean started LensCrafter, which revolutionized the retail eye-care market.

Paul laid out my responsibilities: I would be working on a new line extension called Bold 3, which combined detergent with fabric softener and enzymes for enhanced stain removal. My first task was to help develop the package design, a chance to see how my years studying architecture and design could pay off in a business setting. Back then, there was no computer-assisted design software; everything was done by hand. Good thing I still had my old drafting tools.

By the end of the week, I had created three designs. Dean helped with the details. He and I had a clear favorite, and Paul agreed. Within two weeks, we finalized the design, had mockups made and began the multi-level approval process. I wrote my first memo and submitted it with the package mockup.

The verdict? Approved by the CEO. It was an exhilarating way to begin.

My actual beginning was a couple of weeks prior. At the end of my first day, I was called into the office of Jim VanCleave, Paul's boss, and the promotion manager (later retitled associate advertising manager). After a quick debrief, Jim asked with a slight grin, *"Did you notice everyone here wears long-sleeve white shirts?"* My short-sleeved blue shirt did not meet P&G standards.

I pointed out that it was ninety degrees outside but assured him I'd be purchasing the "uniform" that evening. I then asked, half-jokingly, if he could also tell me what color socks and underwear were expected. Thankfully, he laughed.

P&G Principles

The white shirts were just one of many unwritten P&G customs—but there were also deeply ingrained principles that played a significant role in the company's long-term success. These were not just quirks of corporate culture; they were part of a philosophy that built one of the world's most enduring consumer goods companies.

Founded in 1837 by William Procter and James Gamble, the company had ambitious goals from the start. By the late 1800s, it had adopted a bold objective: **double physical volume every decade**. From 1880 through 1970, P&G remarkably achieved this. It drove dramatic innovations, led to entries into new product categories, and facilitated international expansion. In 1975, then-CEO Ed Harness announced that due to the company's sheer size, achieving the goal was no longer feasible. I remember wondering whether holding on to that goal, no matter how ambitious, might have driven the company to even greater heights.

- **Entry-level hiring only.** P&G does not hire experienced managers from outside the company. Instead, they invest in training all employees "the Procter Way." This approach fosters alignment, builds a cohesive corporate culture, and avoids the disruption that can occur when managers with different approaches to the business are hired.

- **Decisions include top-level input.** At P&G, the CEO is involved in many decisions that other companies would delegate. This helps refine ideas using executive experience and gives young managers rare exposure to senior leadership—benefiting both.

- **Precision in communication.** Internal communications are built around short, structured memos that are consistent in format. The consistency enables efficient decision-making across a complex organization. Each level of management adds a concise summary, and by the time a decision reaches the CEO, the top sheet is often just a paragraph.

  I recently rediscovered a copy of the fabled *Good Book,* a resource filled with examples of how to write internal memos on virtually every subject. It is updated regularly. I was pleased to see that several of my memos had been selected as model correspondence. The Table of Contents for the Good Book is included in the Appendix as Exhibit 6. If the writing in this *Budapest to Boca* story seems well-organized but stiff and dull, you now know who to blame.

- **Training is a key focus of the organization.** It is a crash course in thinking, communicating, and understanding the consumer. P&G people are trained to assume major responsibilities very quickly. Training was the key reason I came to P&G, and I wasn't disappointed.

Immersed in the Brand Assistant Role

I approached my role at P&G the way I had once learned English: full immersion. I absorbed as much as I could about promotion, advertising, sales, and brand management. I studied the *Advertising Good Book*, which laid out how to create, evaluate, and manage winning campaigns.

I developed relationships with senior experts like Norm Levy and Gibby Carey, P&G's advertising authorities, and Jack Claggett, the sales coordinator for PS&D. They offered invaluable insights into the challenges I faced.

The Bold brand group had an excellent year starting in June. The base business exceeded expectations, driven by effective advertising and a solid promotion program that I helped manage. The Bold 3 program was final-ized and entered test markets. The annual February "Budget Meeting," where top management bombards the brand group with questions, went well. Paul, Dean, and I worked seamlessly together, and I learned from both of them.

While my career was off to a strong start, my marriage was not. Most of my workdays ran fourteen to fifteen hours, and Linda's schedule was just as demanding. We occasionally went out to dinner or watched a movie, but our time together was limited. We were both deeply invested in work we enjoyed, and our relationship faded and took a back seat.

The next career milestone was Sales Training, and in July of 1973, I was sent to Louisville, Kentucky. Linda stayed behind.

13

SALES TRAINING IN LOUISVILLE

SALES TRAINING AT PROCTER & GAMBLE IS A PIVOTAL FOUR- TO six-month rotation where future brand managers learn the fundamentals of selling. It's a rite of passage for every P&G marketer—a crash course in the realities of the business, far from the comfort of corporate offices.

Karl Maggard –
District sales manager.
An outstanding
manager who was
responsible for
my successful sales
training.

I was fortunate to be assigned to Louisville, Kentucky, regarded as one of the best locations for sales training. It was close to Cincinnati and led by Sales Manager Karl Maggard, a sharp, no-nonsense leader who took the development of new talent seriously. Karl was an excellent mentor. He would later transition to brand management and end up working for me.

My sales territory included parts of Appalachia, where P&G reps didn't always receive the warmest welcome. Over the years, a parade of Ivy League types passed through these towns, pitching promotions and product plans that didn't always resonate. The accounts had grown weary of new faces.

I had big shoes to fill. The last sales trainee to work under Karl was Jack Wyant, a natural-born salesman who produced record-setting sales during his time in Louisville. Jack was confident, likable, and effortlessly persuasive. I knew following him would be a challenge.

The first few weeks were rough. Several attempts to sell a major Tide promotion fell flat. After a string of unsuccessful calls, Karl spent a couple of days showing me how it was done. He was professional and persuasive—the kind of salesperson I aspired to become. Watching him in action was like seeing a master at work: he listened more than he spoke, anticipated objections, and always found common ground.

Then came the real test: a meeting with Thrifty-Mart, the largest account in the district, with a decision-maker[4] who had no love for P&G. As a statement of his disdain, he refused to carry Tide, P&G's flagship detergent and the top-selling brand in America.

As we started the meeting, the buyer eyed me and asked, *"Are you one of those Eastern Yankees?"* I smiled and replied, *"I am from the East. But I am not a Yankee. I'm from Hungary—a country farther east than even New York."* He was not impressed; but I had one more card to play.

I asked if he knew a young man from Paducah, Kentucky, who had gone to Syracuse with the same dream I had—to play big-time college basketball. He shared the same last name as our grocery executive. The player had struggled with the "Yankee" culture, and I had befriended him. He made the team but did not get to play. He had a successful year academically, in part due to my help with the two common courses we took. He transferred before his sophomore year. We kept in touch and remained friends.

The buyer's expression changed as he realized I was talking about his son. The tone of the meeting softened and became friendlier. Still, there was no Tide order.

---

4 Note: I have avoided naming individuals where their actions or attitudes could be viewed negatively.

The next day, we received a call asking me to come to Thrifty-Mart immediately. My friend had evidently convinced his father that I was, in his words, "a very good guy." Thrifty-Mart not only began stocking Tide but also ran what was thought to be the first buy-one-get-one-free (BOGO) Tide offer, supported by extensive television advertising and two weeks of full-page ads in the local paper, the *Courier-Journal*. In just three weeks, the annual shipments of Tide in the Louisville District nearly doubled. I broke Jack Wyant's record.

Word of the BOGO Tide promotion spread quickly, not just across PS&D, but to other P&G divisions and even other grocery accounts. Within weeks, a dozen major retailers had launched similar campaigns. Upon returning to headquarters, I received a handwritten note from Tom Laco congratulating me on the program's success. I appreciated the gesture, though I knew I was receiving far too much credit for something that was the lucky result of a personal connection. This experience validated a principle I learned from my good friend Dr. Lewis: *Be Kind and Don't Expect Anything in Return.*

During the five months I spent in Louisville, Linda and I made the ninety-mile trip up and down I-75 only about twice a month. We continued to focus on our careers rather than on each other.

14

A NEW ERA IN CINCINNATI

EVEN BEFORE I RETURNED TO CINCINNATI, LINDA AND I BOTH realized that the marriage was not working. With Army basic training and sales training, we had spent nine months apart, with little impact on our relationship. Even when we were together, expressions of feelings and love were nonexistent.

After four years, we decided to end our marriage.

The divorce was entirely amicable. We created a fair process. We listed all our shared assets and bid on them. The total values were equal. The process required minimal legal input. The judge called our approach "very clever" and suggested the attorneys consider it, even if it meant fewer billable hours.

Linda and I wished each other well and went our separate ways. While I still had some feelings for her, I was surprised by how little regret I felt. While somewhat painful, the marriage experience provided learning for the future.

I returned to Cincinnati with a sense of anticipation and relief, a fresh start on every front. I was assigned to the Era brand group as assistant brand manager, a new challenge and an important one.

Era was a liquid detergent still in test market but poised for national expansion. This was a pivotal initiative for Procter & Gamble, as consumer preferences were shifting from powders to liquids. Getting this launch right could determine P&G's competitive position in what was, and remains, one of its most important categories.

My brand manager was Steve Donovan, a strong and thoughtful leader who would eventually rise to become a P&G Vice President. Also on the team were Chuck Lieppe, who had taken me to dinner at the Maissonette during my initial interview trip, and Pat Hill. Chuck, too, would go on to become a VP. All three remained friends long after I had left P&G.

After a few months, Steve was promoted to associate advertising manager, and Chuck stepped into the brand manager role. The team kept its momentum and continued to deliver solid results. I was responsible for managing the promotion program, competitive analysis, especially of Wisk, our key rival, and coordinating national launch schedules with the sales organization.

The role was demanding. I worked sixty to seventy hours a week, driven to improve the business I was responsible for and contribute to the overall success of the brand. I knew I was adding value, and that confidence fueled my passion for the work.

The Good Life in Cincinnati

On the personal side, life was also taking shape. The divorce was final. As part of the settlement, the house was sold, and I moved into a stylish apartment at Queen's Tower, perched on a hill on the city's west side.

From my new place, I had a beautiful view of the Ohio River and downtown Cincinnati. The building had all the amenities: a great restaurant, a pool, tennis courts, and a vibrant community of young professionals. Among them was Doug Falk, who worked with me at P&G. We were good friends and explored the singles scene in Cincinnati together.

Queens Tower was only minutes from the Cincinnati sports stadiums. The excellence of the Cincinnati teams was exciting. The Big Red Machine pulverized the National League in the early 1970s. They won 683 games over the 1970–1976 period. Joe Morgan, Johnny Bench, Tony Perez, and Manager Sparky Anderson were inducted into the Baseball Hall of Fame. Pete Rose would have joined them had it not been for off-the-field issues.

The P&G headquarters was within walking distance of the stadium, and we often caught night games. They won the World Series in 1976, and I was able to root them on from a seat right behind first base.

The Cincinnati Bengals football team was also entertaining. Many of the Bengals were in the Army Reserve Unit I transferred to. Middle linebacker Bill Bergy was the lieutenant, and outside linebacker Jim LeClear was the master sergeant. In 1970, the Bengals drafted Kenny Anderson in the third round of the NFL draft, and he was the cornerstone of the franchise for the next sixteen years. In 1976, they came within a few yards of winning the Super Bowl. It was a ten-minute ride from the Queens Tower to the stadium, and I had season tickets on the forty-yard line. Before the games, I was occasionally able to visit with my Bengal army friends. It made for exciting Sundays.

While my career remained my top priority, I was also building a life that felt balanced and full. I worked long hours but still managed to have an active social life. It was a period of growth, achievement, and enjoyment.

15

Resurrecting the Oldest P&G Detergent Brand

The day I had been waiting for was happening. I got called into advertising manager Charlie Fergusson's office, and he informed me that I was being promoted to brand manager on Oxydol. It was three years and two months from my first day, ahead of the typical three-and-a-half- to four-year standard. He said this was an opportunity to use my entrepreneurial bent and creativity to resurrect the brand, which was now a shadow of its former self.

I was excited not only about achieving the brand manager position, but also about the support I received from Charlie. He was a brilliant and highly creative manager. You seldom left his office without a couple of great new ideas. I left Charlie's office highly motivated and ready to meet the challenges facing Oxydol.

What made it even more special was that I reported to associate advertising manager Paul Geissler, my first boss at P&G, and someone I admired and respected. It was a full-circle moment.

Occidental is a historic laundry detergent brand created in 1914 by the Thomas Hadley Company in Newcastle, England. It became a leading brand in England and was expanded to the United States. P&G purchased the brand in 1927. It was P&G's first laundry soap product.

During the 1930s, Occidental gained widespread recognition by sponsoring the Ma Perkins radio show, that is considered the first American soap opera. In the late 30s, the brand's name was changed to Oxydol. The brand was marketed as a soap that made clothes white without bleaching. Oxydol commercials emphasized saving time and effort in laundry, particularly as washing machines became more prevalent in American homes. However, with the introduction of P&G's new detergent, Tide, in the mid-1950s, Oxydol began to experience declining sales.

The Oxydol brand was indeed in trouble when I became brand manager in the fall of 1974, with a share at an all-time low, slightly below 2 percent. In about a third of the country, the share was well below 1 percent, and the brand was in danger of being discontinued, by most accounts. Fortunately, under the leadership of the previous brand managers, Jan VanHorne, followed by Rich Edler, a major restaging program was developed and was about to go into test market. It included an improved product with color-safe bleach, new advertising, and an impactful introductory promotion program.

The test markets significantly outperformed objectives, and we expanded the program to all the targeted districts. By the end of 1975, virtually all districts had a minimum 2 percent share. Together with my team, we refined the messaging, enhanced the promotions, and ensured flawless execution of the restaging. Jan, who had accepted an international assignment, and Rich did not get the credit they deserved despite our efforts to include them in our communications with management.

With the recovery of the Oxydol brand in hand, I was ready for the next step: copy supervisor, a position responsible for advertising across three or four brands. I was made Copy Supervisor at the beginning of 1976, continuing to work with Geisler. We developed effective ad campaigns for all the brands we managed.

I was also responsible for coordinating the strategy on light-duty liquids. The team consisted of over twenty individuals, with representatives from sales, manufacturing, advertising services, and the brands. As the team leader, I was involved in all aspects of the category. Ultimately, we established the foundation for a new brand and implemented a major cost-saving program, delivering $40 million in annual savings.

All was well. I really liked the people I was working with, felt I was contributing meaningfully to the business, and genuinely enjoyed myself outside of work. My horses were winning, and I enjoyed watching them at Latonia, the local harness track. I was receiving regular job offers, but I wasn't interested in pursuing any of them.

General Foods was the most persistent. About every eighteen months, they would approach me with a new offer—each at a higher level and typically with a significant increase in compensation. My answer remained the same: *"I'm very happy with where I am, what I'm doing, and who I'm doing it with."* Little did I know that two special women were about to make my life even better—and certainly more interesting.

16

PEG AND GAIN

PEG WYANT WAS A PIONEER—AND SOMEWHAT OF A REBEL.

Peg joined P&G in 1967, when women were rarely considered for management roles. She was the first female brand manager at Procter & Gamble and may very well have been the first female executive at any major public company.

She was competent, confident, and fearless—a true trailblazer. She married Jack Wyant, who had worked for her, and by then they had two children. Her second child, Missy, was born on December 7, 1975, and as 1976 began, she was on a three-month maternity leave. Even on sabbatical, she kept a close eye on the brands she oversaw as an associate advertising manager.

One of those brands was Gain detergent—and it quickly became her most pressing challenge. Gain featured a new enzyme detergent that delivered superior stain removal. The problem? Internally, there were growing concerns that this could threaten Tide, the market leader. At the same time, rumors were swirling about the enzyme causing health issues among employees at the manufacturing plant.

Whether justified or not, these concerns created a sense of emergency. Management decided that the enzymes needed to be removed immediately, and the brand needed to be restaged behind an entirely new positioning.

Normally, this would require an approximately eighteen-month process involving analysis, written proposals, test markets, and multiple layers of approvals. But Peg had a different idea.

In her terrific book *One Red Shoe*, she describes her rather brave and unusual approach:

> *If we were going to save the brand, we would need to change its course dramatically and now. I made an appointment with Sandy Weiner, the PS&D Advertising Manager, to ask for agreement to a 90-day period during which the brand group would have absolute freedom to take any and all actions with the product, the packaging, and the advertising. Giving me and the brand manager complete control. To understand how revolutionary this request was, imagine a top-down managed company where every decision—even changing a single line of copy on the package—required agreement of the Executive Committee which would meet every Tuesday at 10:00 am on the hallowed 11TH floor.*

> *Once more, to enhance the probability of success, I requested the assignment of the brand manager of my choice—Tom Herskovits. It was a bold request, given that Tom was #1 in the division hit parade of brand managers. If we had a shot at turning the ship—the barge actually—around, we needed power, control and top talent. And no bureaucratic entanglements.*

It should be noted that my #1 designation came after Peg was already my sister-in-law. She did, however, ask for me before we knew each other, foreshadowing the most important connection of my life.

As usual, Peg got everything she asked for.

What Peg didn't know was the internal discussion that preceded my Gain assignment.

Sandy Weiner, who had recently become advertising manager, was not just my mentor—he was also a friend. He invited me to dinner at a cozy spot in Wyoming, the Cincinnati suburb where he lived, to discuss my future.

Before the Gain "emergency," I had evidently been one of two candidates for the Tide brand manager role, the crown jewel of brand assignments at P&G. Sandy reminded me that nearly every P&G CEO, including John Smale and John Pepper, had once held the Tide job.

He asked, "*Wouldn't you be excited to run the biggest brand in the company?*" It was a moment where I could give a corporate answer or an honest one. I chose honesty.

"*Tide is like the Queen Elizabeth—lots of onlookers, hard to steer, and almost too big to control,*" I said. "*It's tough to be the captain when four admirals are watching your every move. I want to captain a fleet of speedboats—and drive the lead boat.*"

Sandy, always quick-witted, told me to cut the maritime metaphors—but he understood. While he had some reservations about my passing up Tide, he acknowledged that the visibility and urgency of the Gain assignment might propel my career forward even faster.

He suggested I talk to Peg before making a decision.

Of course, this was a formality. We both knew it wasn't really my decision to make.

Though Peg was still on maternity leave, she came into the office to meet with me. While we hadn't worked together before. I knew her reputation: very smart, creative, and action-oriented. Our meeting confirmed

> *Sandy Weiner was a brilliant marketer. He was one of the most talented corporate executives I have encountered. He was creative, intuitive, with an engaging personality. He was my mentor and my friend. I was devastated when he passed away due to cancer, likely caused by the pipe he was seldom without. I am convinced he would have become P&G's CEO.*

it. I liked her immediately, and I shared her excitement about what we could do together.

Our advertising agency was Doyle Dane Bernbach (DDB). They were new to P&G and new to Gain. They were the "hot" agency known for creating groundbreaking advertising, while P&G was known for its strict formula approach. DDB was challenged to think "outside of the box" to create a persuasive positioning that would build Gain long-term. The first couple of meetings we had with DDB were disastrous. The first meeting was with the brand, our account group, and creative team counterparts.

Marvin Honig led their creative team and declared that there was nothing special about Gain, and he could not see producing any persuasive advertising. While Bob Levinson, who was not in the meeting, was DDB's creative director, Marvin was viewed as one of the top two or three creatives on Madison Avenue. He was the creator of award-winning ads for Alka-Seltzer, Volkswagen, and many other clients. He was already in the Advertising Hall of Fame. The Account Group tried to minimize the negative impact of Marvin's tirade and left quickly.

About two weeks later, DDB returned, and this meeting featured more senior representation, including Bob Levinson and Bill Bernbach, the founder of the agency. Peg had promised them we would produce any commercials they recommended, which should have stimulated the kind of ingenious creative that DDB was known for. The "Frog" commercial was produced. When Peg saw it, she made herself very clear, declaring, "Scrap it!" I agreed.

I could sense that Marvin, their star creative, also agreed and probably had nothing to do with Frog—he was shaking his head and rolling his eyes. While the Agency was wasting time creating advertising without a solid positioning, the brand group was exploring every possible approach.

The attribute that kept surfacing was smell and freshness—Gain smelled fresh, and this was proof of cleanliness. In focus groups, where we asked consumers to discuss laundry, the brand, and the ad, reinforced the potential of the idea. Peg and I tried to get the agency to work with the concept, but they pretty much rejected it.

After the second contentious meeting, I took Marvin to lunch. I asked him where he was from, and he answered that he was born in Kansas but grew up in Louisville, Kentucky. I relayed the story of Tide and Thrifty-Mart, and suddenly, lightning struck again. I knew that I was about to make Marvin a lifelong friend.

Marvin Honig: Talented creative at Doyle Dane, Burnbach. Creative responsible for the successful Gain advertising campaign and later for the award-winning Frusen Glädjé advertising.

"Do you by chance know a Mrs. Honig who lived on the South side of Louisville, next to the library?" I asked. *"That's my mom,"* Marvin answered with anticipation in his voice. How does he know my mother?

There is a Hebrew word "bashert" that means that something was meant to be. This was clearly bashert.

When I was in basic training in Ft. Knox, Kentucky, just outside Louisville, in the fall of 1971, soldiers were allowed to go off-base to celebrate the most important Jewish holidays, Rosh Hashanah and Yom Kippur, with area volunteers. I visited the Honig house on three occasions, and his mother and I really liked each other. She was a sweet lady who reminded me of Kato, who took care of me while my mom was in jail.

Instantaneously, attitudes changed, and Marvin began to recognize the potential of the freshness positioning. Meanwhile, Peg was also reading the "riot act" to Mr. Levinson, and he, too, was beginning to see the potential of freshness.

A couple of weeks later, at a meeting attended by agency founder Bill Burnbach, Bob Levinson, and Marwin, DDB presented a delightful ad campaign highlighting freshness as proof of clean positioning. The announcer in the woods and the star housewife enjoying the freshness of her Gain-washed laundry had to be appealing to consumers. I was the first to give my opinion on the positioning and the advertising and was appropriately nervous. A smile and a thumbs-up, which only I could see, from Peg gave me confidence that my approval was justified. I delivered my strong support of the advertising, and Peg followed with her positive input.

A few days later, we presented the whole Gain program:

- Two new ads built on the freshness positioning

- The new no-enzyme, freshness-enhanced product

- A new, brighter package design, and

- An impactful trial-oriented promotion program

The entire program was approved, and all our top managers were enthusiastic about it.

In under 90 days, we created a completely revamped brand. The brand initially stabilized, and, over time, outperformed virtually all P&G detergents. Today, Gain is P&G's number two brand with sales over $1 billion.

Fifty years later, the freshness positioning remains the core message of the brand. Peg and I were applauded and rewarded. She ultimately became head of Procter & Gamble Strategy, reporting directly to CEO and Chairman John Smale, and I got promoted to associate advertising manager (AAM) in early 1977.

17

THE MATCH AND THE BLACKOUT

PEG AND I WORKED WELL TOGETHER, AND SHE CERTAINLY accelerated my career. But her greatest contribution wasn't professional—it was personal. As she got to know me better, she became convinced that her sister-in-law Rita would be a perfect match for me. It was also the solution to P&G's growing concern about the continual stream of competitive job offers I was receiving. As she recounts in her *One Red Shoe* book:

> *I decided he—focused, disciplined and brilliant—was the perfect match for Rita, Jack's sister—fun and bubbly, with the most compelling and likable personality. Company Personnel reviews were serious happening. The Group Product Manager (me in this case) presents recommendations for their people to the Advertising Manager, vice presidents of the division and vice presidents of personnel and advertising. In the review following our positive Gain experience, the serious senior men were debating what assignment would be effective in keeping Tom with the company for the long term. I listened to their meanderings for a while. Then I interrupted the conversation: what Tom needs is a wife and two kids. I'll fix that. They didn't know what to say.*

Dating my boss's sister-in-law was not high on my "to-do" list. Dating Jack Wyant's sister did not even make the list. While Jack was a good-looking guy, sharp and professional, his bow tie and Brooks Brothers style did not signal a sister that I would relate to. But after almost a year of Peg's coaxing, I relented. We agreed to meet for lunch in a restaurant in Kentucky. I figured that just in case I did not want to be seen, across the river was safe. Rita was a flight attendant for Capitol International Airways, and she had her own exit strategy. If things did not go well, she could make a quick exit to the Cincinnati airport, which is actually located in Kentucky.

I was at the restaurant first and was scanning the entrance when Rita walked in. Let's just say she instantly ascended to the top of my list. She was beautiful in a light orange dress that highlighted her graceful figure. It took only a brief conversation to recognize that this girl was extremely bright with, as Peg had tried to tell me, a most compelling, likable personality. Our discussions covered a wide range of topics, including global issues, women's rights, and the state of Cincinnati sports. When I finally glanced at my watch, it was almost three, and she was late for her flight to Las Vegas, and I was late for a meeting. I paid the bill and gave her $10 to bet in Las Vegas. When I got back to the office, Peg was waiting anxiously for a report. I covered it in one word—WOW!

A few weeks went by, and I kept asking Peg about my $10. I was anxious to reconnect. The following Saturday morning, my phone rang, and it was Rita. *"Sorry for not calling, and very sorry for losing your $10. I am in town for a couple of days and would love to get together,"* she said

This now required some quick thinking.

I had a visitor from Los Angeles in town for a few days. I made a flimsy business excuse and drove her to the airport. She was out of town by 2:00 p.m., and Rita and I were out to dinner by 6:00. We again had a great time and agreed to meet in New York the week after. She was flying in from Europe, and I was coming in for an agency meeting.

It was July 13, 1977, a date we still celebrate. The plan for the evening was the off-Broadway show *Vanities*, followed by dinner at

Sardi's. I reserved a limo to take Rita to Queens to stay at her friend's house after dinner.

Vanities was the story of three Texas high school cheerleaders. It starred Kathy Bates and was one of the longest-running off-Broadway shows ever. It had three acts, which was unusual for New York theater.

We were in the third act, enjoying the show. When all the lights suddenly went out. No one knew what was happening. One of the traits I inherited from my mother is the tendency to instantly imagine the worst-case scenario. We were on the far west side of Manhattan, not a particularly safe neighborhood. My first thought was that we were about to be mugged by hoodlums who had killed the electricity. After a few minutes of stunned silence, a theater employee came out on stage holding a candle.

"This is a city-wide blackout," he said. *"Con Edison has indicated that power is not expected to be restored for at least a couple of hours."*

He suggested that we leave the theater by candlelight, led by the theater staff.

18

~~Surviving~~ Enjoying the Blackout

What an eerie sight. Total darkness, with the only light from the cigarettes of those sitting on the stairs adjacent to the sidewalk. Rita started engaging with the folks behind the cigarettes. *"I have $1,200 in my wallet, I am not interested in others knowing that I'm here,"* I told her. We could hardly make out the sidewalk in front of us, but we increased our pace and stopped talking.

We walked into Sardi's, and they were not in a position to feed anybody this evening. We also had no way to contact the hired limo, as cell phones were not available until a few years later. So much for The Plan.

We agreed that it made sense to go to my hotel and wait for the lights to go on. As usual, I was staying at the Park Lane Hotel on 57th Street and Central Park. The good news was that we only had about half a mile to go. The not-so-good news was that I was staying in my usual room, 4608, on the forty-sixth floor of a hotel now without a working elevator.

There was a faint light in the stairwell from the hotel's generator. Rita and I looked at each other, and it seemed neither one of us wanted to admit that we would be unable to make it. "Will you carry me upstairs if I can't make it?" I asked sheepishly. That broke the ice, and we started walking up the stairs. About halfway up, we took a break, then pushed on until we reached room 4608. It was 11 p.m. on Thursday, and it quickly became clear that Rita would have to stay until power was restored. Around 11:30, the intercom blared: *"Power wouldn't be back until late Friday or even Saturday."*

We had a very relaxing Friday. While we had no electricity, we very much enjoyed each other's company. Thirty-six hours without air conditioning, running water, or a change of clothes (for Rita), and you get to know the person you're with. It's fair to say that while the physical attraction between us was strong, we both came to genuinely appreciate each other as people during this ordeal.

When we woke up on Saturday, the power came back on. We called to get tickets to the play *Chicago*, went out for something to eat, and then headed to the theater. We left at intermission and returned to the Park Lane, this time able to take the elevator to the forty-sixth floor. We enjoyed each other more than the play.

Rita likes to tell the story that when she got in a cab to the airport on Sunday morning, the cab driver asked her, *"What did you do during the blackout?"* She replied, *"For the first time in my life, I fell in love and met the man that I think I could live with for the rest of my life."* She has been looking for the cab driver ever since to be able to tell him that she, in fact, married that guy.

For me, the situation was somewhat less clear. Having been divorced and enjoying the single life, I was committed to maintaining my independence. Yet here was a woman whom I was not only very much attracted to but also someone I really enjoyed being with. Was this love?

Rita was back in town in a couple of weeks, and our next date was a three-day jaunt to Hawaii. In those days, a lead flight attendant could easily get you on the plane without a ticket. We had a great time, including the opportunity to see the original Ink Spots perform. We continued to have great times the rest of the summer, including a weekend in French Lick, Indiana, and multiple trips to New York.

Another one of our favorite activities was an evening at Latonia, the harness track located next to the airport in Kentucky. While I no longer owned horses, I had a perfect table by the finish line and a designated waitress named Rita, who would always take very good care of me. She also provided judgment on my dates to the track. She would stand behind them and rate them thumbs up, even, or down. While I had a couple of evens, the rest were all down—she had very high standards. Then came Rita, who not only received the first thumbs-up rating but got an enthusiastic two thumbs up.

19

The Wyants

The very positive feelings I had were not limited to Rita alone. I was very impressed by her entire family. Her father, Jack, and mother, Margaret, were both deaf, the result of childhood diseases. Jack loved sports, so we always had a lot to chat about, communicating with each other by writing on his notepad. He was an amazing guy. He worked at the nearby Diebold plant and ran an office cleaning business in the evenings. He supported and raised four incredible children, all of whom hold college degrees. He was respected by all who knew him.

Margaret was warm and friendly with a brilliant smile and a vibrant personality. She had her first child, Jack, at the age of twenty, and Rita two and a half years later. At that point, they took measures to keep the family as a comfortable foursome. But seventeen years later, nature intervened, and to everyone's surprise, Margaret's discomfort was diagnosed as a pregnancy. Kent was born on April 21, 1966. They decided to have another child, and Andrew was born on November 22, 1968.

Kent was eleven and Andrew was nine years old when I first met Rita. They were amazing kids: bright, articulate, and well-mannered. They were a true blessing for their parents. Much as Judy and I were a positive influence on our stepfather, Nathan, the boys were a major plus in my relationship with Rita.

My relationship with Jack, Rita's brother, developed slowly. It took him a while to recognize that Peg was right, Rita and I were perfect for each other. Jack had recently made a career move to venture capital, starting the Blue Chip Fund, Cincinnati's first venture organization. I was one of Jack's first investors and also became a resource in the difficult process of evaluating potential investment ideas. We respected each other's opinions, and over time, Jack and I became close friends.

Peg and Jack have four amazing kids. Jackie is now the squash coach for both men's and women's teams at the University of Pennsylvania. He was a squash All-American and captain of the Princeton team. His sister, Missy, followed him to Princeton and was also an All-American—the first brother/sister combination to be All-Americans at the same time in a sport. Today, Missy is one of the leading realtors in San Francisco.

Tim attended Harvard, played soccer, and was also captain of the squash team. He now leads The Squash Education Alliance that mentors underprivileged kids utilizing squash as its focus. Chris, not to be outdone by his siblings, went to Yale and was a strong performer on the squash team. He has worked in investment banking and held leadership positions in Barack Obama's campaigns, as well as in the creation and operation of his library. Jack and Peg have eleven very talented grandkids.

Many of the traits that make Rita so special are shared by all the Wyants. At Jackie's wedding to his lovely wife Amelia, I gave a toast that summarized what it was like to be hooked up with a Wyant:

Toast to Amelia and Jackie at Their Wedding

"My name is Tom Herskovits, and I have been hitched to a Wyant longer than any person in this room except for Peg. I feel a responsibility to let you, Amelia, know what you are in for. I will say that you could talk to Peg, but she is finally marrying off her eldest, so I do not think she is an objective and reliable source on this issue.

There are four primary points that I would like to highlight. First, is communication. Wyants are communicators. They do not need Bluetooth with their Blackberries—it is built into their ears. They call you, they call each other, and they will call all of your family, anytime, anywhere, and about anything. [Note: this was in the pre-Zoom era. Zoom has significantly increased the Wyants' communication.]

The second area, and this is serious, is that Wyants go to everything. We are talking about kindergarten graduations, parents' days at elementary school, basketball games, dance recitals, high school graduations, and so on. Now, there are about 12 Wyants, with many more on the way. So, if you figure 18 events per person, you are talking about over 200 events, or about one-fifth of your waking hours over the next five years. And do not think you are protected just because you are in Philadelphia—the farther the event, the more likely they are to show up.

Third is energy. The Energizer Bunny has nothing on a Wyant. Parties that last till 4 am, seven-day trips in three days and on and on. And you would think that over the years they would wear out, but they don't ... they keep on ticking.

Finally, all the Wyants are committed to "Make the Best of It." No matter what, they will find something positive even in the most negative situation. As your husband's great-grandfather Pal would say, "Seldom Have a Bad Day."

Loyal, family-oriented, all good-looking and intelligent ... they produce fabulous offspring, and they attract brilliant, great-looking mates. The one thing you can count on is that they will make your life fun and exciting.

20

Judy, My Mother, & Margo

My sister, Judy, and I have had a close relationship throughout our lives. We agreed that each of us would have what we called "veto power" over potential mates. I was thrilled when Len Wizmur came on the scene. He was bright, good-looking, and clearly smitten with my sister. He had a locker right next to Judy in law school, and amazingly, they were both delivered by the same doctor in Budapest. It was after my approval that Judy brought Len home to meet our parents.

Rita and I followed the same approach. We set up dinner with Judy and Len near their home in Mt. Laurel, New Jersey. We had a delightful evening, and Judy and Rita became instant friends. Thanksgiving dinner was set for Rita and me at my parents' home in Clifton.

While my mom was certainly impressed with Rita, there were questions. A flight attendant who is traveling all over the world? Deaf parents? Would their children be deaf? Is Tom just on the rebound? While my mom was happy that I seemed ready to give up my commitment to independence, she was not sure Rita was the answer.

Rita had a very busy flight schedule over the next month, reaching her annual maximum miles by the end of November. The free time in December took her to a vegan, no-phone or TV yoga retreat in Bonita Springs, Florida, a relaxing, quiet departure from her very high-octane life.

I was busy in Cincinnati preparing for the annual P&G budget meetings. My parents were at their condo in Hallandale, Florida. Rita and I had been there previously, and she called to ask whether I thought it would be a good idea for her to visit my parents. I said, Sure.

When she arrived at the condominium, she saw my parents at the pool with a couple of ladies. As she greeted my parents, it was clear that they did not recognize her. She said, *"I'm Tom's friend and I am on my way to the Miami airport and will be flying to London this evening. I thought I would stop and say hello."* My mother remembered and introduced Rita to my aunt Hilda and her friend Margo.

In the next instant, Margo jumped up from her seat in sudden recognition, hugging Rita and yelling, "Rita, My Rita? Don't you recognize me?" As a flight attendant for Capitol International Airlines, Rita flew about 100 flights per year on a Stretch DC-8 that was usually filled to the 252-seat capacity. It would be difficult for a person to remember a couple from the over 50,000 people on her flights since she encountered Margo and her husband two years ago.

As Margo kept talking, Rita did remember. On a charter flight organized by the Bar Association from JFK to Paris, Margo and her husband were assigned two seats that were already occupied. Rita sat them in the flight attendant seats and assured them that she would take care of them during the flight.

Each time Rita passed their seats, she dropped off a miniature liquor bottle. She then sat next to them and described many of her life experiences, including her deaf parents, her younger brothers, the charters into Vietnam that brought soldiers to and from the battlefields, the Vietnamese family that she sponsored and who lived in their basement for almost a year. As the morning sun was coming up, Rita noticed a group of Orthodox Jews looking for a place to pray. She cordoned off a section of the plane to give them privacy.

Margo, last name unknown—her chance encounter on a charter flight and ten brief minutes poolside had a major impact on our lives.

Margo and her husband were enchanted. They begged Rita to take their son's number and at least arrange to meet him. She indicated that she avoided any relationships stemming from her professional career and that she was too busy with the Vietnamese family she sponsored and with her involvement with her young brothers. She thought for sure that she would never see the couple again; yet here was Margo lecturing my parents.

"Is this the girl that your son wants to marry? You're the luckiest people—I would kill to have her in our family." While Rita never saw Margo after that encounter, she played a meaningful role in solidifying my parents' positive impression of Rita. That evening, they called. They confirmed that Rita stopped by. They thought she was fabulous, and I would be a fool not to marry her. This was another example of Dr. Lewis's "Be Kind and Don't Expect Anything in Return" edict working wonders.

21

ENGAGEMENT, MARRIAGE, A DISAPPOINTMENT, AND A THRILL

WHILE I WAS PLEASED THAT MY PARENTS APPROVED OF RITA, I was still somewhat hesitant to give up my independence. However, as Rita and I spent time together over the next few months, I had no doubts that I was ready to commit. I also had three very powerful women—my mom, my sister, and Peg—encouraging me to make the move. Peg, who is not known for subtlety, gave Rita and me a holiday present—a canvas tote. She gave me a sheet of iron-on initials. "What's it going to be, Tom? RW or RWH on that tote.

I proposed on March 30, my birthday and my parents' anniversary. We were married on July 2nd, 1978, in a beautiful ceremony at the Valley Temple in the Cincinnati suburb of Wyoming. It was officiated by an impressive young rabbi, Sol Greenberg. The ceremony was followed by a reception at Jack and Peg's house on Signal Hill, Cincinnati. It was a scorching hot day, and by the end of the day, many of us were in their backyard pool.

Our honeymoon cruise took us to various islands in the Caribbean. On our second day at sea, we called our realtor and friend, Maddy Cohen, and made an offer on a house we had seen in Amberley Village, a fashionable suburb of Cincinnati. It was a custom house built for what must have been a very particular couple. As a student of architecture, I appreciated the many unique features of the house. Two days later, we received confirmation that our offer had been accepted. This was hardly a "starter" house, and my detailed budget calculations indicated that we could just about afford it, utilizing the remnants of my Record Runner "fortune" that I had saved for a rainy day.

Back to Work

When I got back to the office, I had a message from Mr. Laco to see him. He wanted to congratulate me on my marriage. When I told him about the house, he asked whether I had committed to a mortgage. I had not. He set up a meeting with a Fifth Third Bank VP and I secured a mortgage commitment almost 2 percent lower than my bank—a clear example of Procter & Gamble's influence in Cincinnati.

Rita continued to work for Capitol for a few more months, and I was busy, engrossed in my job as AAM. I continued to coordinate our light-duty liquid strategy as well as the emerging liquid detergent market. While my brands were doing well, I was developing issues with a couple of managers who were relatively new to PS&D. The differences I had with my new colleagues marked the first time at P&G that I didn't feel fully aligned with those I worked with and for. I was convinced that while we were dealing with complex issues, I was right, and John Pepper, the PS&D executive vice president, agreed with me.

As I was contemplating an offer to be COO of Bordon's in Columbus, Ohio, I was reassured by John that I was getting close to being promoted to advertising manager and that the issues I raised would be addressed.

I appreciated John's candor. John Pepper was, and remains, a wonderful human being and a very impressive, competent executive. He rounds out the trio I idolized at P&G, alongside Tom Laco and Sandy Weiner. While I did not have the kind of personal relationship that I had with Tom and Sandy, I nevertheless had the same level of respect and admiration for him. John eventually became CEO and chairman of Procter & Gamble.

I passed on the Bordon's opportunity, as an exciting family event became my focus.

Kathryn Arrives and Meets Kato.

In the spring of 1979, we found out that Rita was pregnant. She retired from Capitol, and we celebrated her $2,350 retirement pension. Rita had an easy pregnancy until the last two months, when things got tough with preeclampsia, keeping her bedridden. She also spent two days in labor before the doctors convinced us to do a C-section. I spent the whole two days at her bedside, often playing 500 rum when she was able.

Kathryn was born on November 8, 1979. At first, they gave her to Rita to hold, and I got her about five minutes later. She was gorgeous right from the beginning. She had beautiful features and striking red hair. Even as a newborn, she was looking around, seemingly evaluating the scene around her. This was a harbinger of things to come. Kathryn was named after Kato, who so lovingly took care of me in Szombathely.

Kathryn was an amazing child. She began speaking well before her first birthday and was reading by the time she was two. Her pre-school teacher suggested that we have her tested. At the age of three, it was very clear that she was, and would continue to be, far advanced for her age. We were advised not to move her too quickly up the academic ladder to ensure that she would be comfortable socially.

Those first months with Kathryn were magical. Every day brought something new. In March, right after the P&G budget season, Rita had a surprise birthday gift. *"Start packing, we are going to see Kato again. She needs to meet the person who will carry her name for the next generation."*

Rita had arranged a very emotional visit a few months after we were married. She knew how important it would be to be with Béla and Kato before our time to hug, kiss, and thank them in person would run out. It was truly gratifying to be reunited with them after almost twenty-five years of separation. The visit culminated in Béla announcing that now that he had seen me grown, successful, with a beautiful wife, living in a free country, he could die in peace. He passed away within weeks after we returned to the States.

Now we were there again to introduce Kathryn to her namesake. Landing in Tel Aviv, Edna and Judith, the daughters of Erno Fleisher, my biological father's best friend, drove us to Erno's home in Jerusalem. They had a beautiful three-story home just a few short blocks away from the Western Wall, which is the last remnant of the Second Temple, destroyed by the Romans in 70 CE.

We spent the day engrossed in stories about my father and my time in Szombathely. Erno recounted how he waited for his best friend and his family in Vienna, and they never came. It was one of the great disappoint-

ments of his life.

We also talked about my time in Szombathely and how everyone was surprised by how readily Béla accepted me. Erno reminded me that although I never beat Béla in chess, I never

lost to him.

The next morning, we visited Kato. Once again, the memories came rushing back—the terrace, her delicious dinners, and the endless chess matches with Béla.

She continued to laugh at my "six-year-old" Hungarian speech and we reminisced about Béla and my role in his life and his in mine. However, the focus of this visit was the little girl on the couch. It was clear that Kato was visibly moved to have a namesake. She and Kathryn connected in a way that is hard to describe, but the love that flowed between this bright little child and this wonderful woman was unmistakable. I will be forever grateful to Rita for the precious moments we had.

22

THE AAM DILEMNA AND GENERAL FOODS COMES CALLING.... AGAIN

THE TRIP TO ISRAEL WAS A NEEDED BREAK FROM THE STRESSFUL budget season. The role of the AAM in the budget meeting process was difficult and somewhat conflicting. There was a need to ensure that the brands were prepared for the meeting and an obligation to provide upper management with the key issues for each brand.

I was now entering my third year as AAM. In many ways, this was the least satisfying position I held at Procter & Gamble. The brand managers ran the brands, copy supervisors managed advertising, and the advertising manager and division manager determined the overall strategies for the division.

Dirk Jager, Neil DeFeo, Greg Lawton, and Ross Love formed an excellent management group that made my life as AAM easy. Proud of the fact that they all got promoted to higher positions.

I had three excellent brand managers working for me, including Dirk Yager, who later became P&G's CEO, Neil DeFeo, who became a very successful executive and venture capitalist, and Greg Lawton, who, after leaving P&G, had senior management positions at Johnson's Wax and was president of NuTone Inc. Ross Love was my copy supervisor. His judgment on advertising was impeccable. Ross later became VP of advertising services for all of P&G.

With all this talent in our group, there was little need for the training or the quality control functions that were often the focus of the associate ad manager position. I was at my best facing complex challenges that required out-of-the-box innovative thinking and focused, all-out effort. I did not identify such opportunities.

In retrospect, my attitude mimicked P&G's arguably unacceptable stance that we could no longer double volume in the 1970s. I should have pushed harder to identify and implement transformative initiatives within my areas of responsibility.

The business issues that I had previously been concerned about were still unresolved. We were not pursuing liquid versions of our key laundry brands, particularly Tide, and we were not as aggressive as I thought we should be on Dawn. As the coordinator of light-duty liquids, I was convinced that the grease-fighting positioning of Dawn, supported by patented technology, would be our strongest long-term platform. Competitors like Palmolive were threatening to beat us in the marketplace with a barrage of marketing spending. I was unable to have an immediate impact on this issue, although over time, Dawn has become the leading dishwashing liquid.

It was with this background that I fielded my biennial call from Bill Dordelman, an executive vice president at General Foods. This time, the conversation was different. Bill said he wasn't offering a lateral move, luring me with compensation alone. He had an opportunity for me to become president of General Foods' Breakfast Foods Division, overseeing Post Cereals, Log Cabin Syrup, and other developing breakfast brands. He believed it was the most exciting

Bill Dordelman—General Foods executive most responsible for my departure from P&G to run the Breakfast Foods Division of General Foods.

leadership opportunity at GF and that I was the right person to seize it. As we spoke, two brand fact books were on route to my home.

A Night to Remember in the Big Apple

On Thursday afternoon, a limo took Rita, Kathryn, and me to Cincinnati's Lunken Airport, where a GF Falcon 50 jet awaited. We were greeted by a member of the GF flight department who served as our private flight attendant.

Upon landing at Westchester Airport, we were met by two limos. In one were Bill Dordelman and his wife, Barbara. In the other limo was Sandy, who introduced herself as Kathryn's babysitter. Sandy took Kathryn and our luggage to our hotel.

Rita and I joined Bill and Barbara for the ride to Manhattan. We were treated to great seats for West Side Story, the high-energy play that won the Tony Award for best revival that year. This was followed by dinner at one of my favorite restaurants, the Four Seasons, home to the world-renowned Hungarian chef Georges Lang, the chef my stepfather, Nathan, tried to emulate. We had a spectacular meal, with little talk of business. That would come the next day. Returning to the Ryetown Hilton, we found roses and a welcome note from General Foods Chairman Jim Ferguson. A fitting end to a truly remarkable evening.

A Big Opportunity and a Big Decision

Kathryn woke at 6 am the next morning, which meant we were up too. Over coffee, I reviewed my notes on Post Cereal and mentally rehearsed the day ahead. Today was going to be a marathon—a string of interviews with the top brass of General Foods.

First stop: Bill Dordelman.

We skipped pleasantries. Bill leaned forward, clasping his hands.

"Let's talk about the things that might keep you at P&G," he said.

I didn't hesitate. *"Leaving mentors like Sandy Weiner, Tom Laco, and John Pepper—that's my biggest concern."*

Bill nodded.

"Fair. But you'd have strong leaders here too—Phil Smith, Erv Shames. You could count on them."

I filed that away. The names would come up again.

Next up: Bill Korab, President of the Breakfast Foods Division.

Surprisingly, our conversation was relaxed. Bill revealed that he'd be moving to a new role within the year. If I proved myself as chief marketing officer, I'd become division president. He joked, *"If the business does well, you get the credit. If it doesn't, I get the blame."*

Bill Korab—instrumental in my successful transition into GF. Instructive about the culture of GF and very helpful in introducing me to key people in the business.

Korab had a dry humor I liked. We dove into Post Cereal's potential. I shared my early impressions: *"Three things jump out: launch new products, upgrade the nutrition, and improve execution in both advertising and promotions.* Bill leaned forward. *"I agree—all three. And here's where I think we can push each even further."* By the time I left, I was already thinking, Yes, I could work with this guy.

Then came Erv Shames.

He was exactly as I'd heard—understated, thoughtful, analytical. His nickname "The Professor" fit. *"Tell me about your style,"* he asked, *"and not just the résumé version."*

I discussed team-building, pushing for creative solutions and big ideas, and overcoming bureaucracy when necessary. Erv nodded occasionally, jotting a note or two.

"Division presidents here have more autonomy than at P&G," he explained. *"We're moving away from the Harvard MBA approach. We want leaders who think like entrepreneurs."*

He reminded me of Sandy Weiner—humble, insightful, and quietly confident. He actually went on to teach at the University of Virginia's Darden School of Business.

Lunch with Korab was lighter—sports, politics, travel. We'd covered the business in the morning, and it was clear the personal chemistry was there.

Phil Smith was next. He was the soon-to-be CEO, former Marine Corps captain and fighter pilot. Direct. To the point. *"We want aggressive, creative leaders,"* he said. *"Entrepreneurs in corporate clothing. You'll get earlier general management responsibility here—and more balance in your life."*

I believed him.

Finally: Jim Ferguson, Chairman and CEO.

Tall, imposing, and thoughtful—like me, he had started at P&G. He valued brand management but preferred GF's decentralized approach. *"My focus is strategy and leadership development,"* he said. *"Not packaging details or ad copy—that's your job."*

The alignment of messaging from each interview told me this was not exploratory. A decision to try to hire me had already been made.

Back to Bill Dordelman.

He laid the offer on the table—division president-level compensation, relocation assistance, and home buyout. A clear vote of confidence. I was excited about the opportunity not only because of the increased responsibility, but also the focus on entrepreneurship. Their description of the leader they were seeking was the way that I viewed myself.

That night, Rita and I drove to my parents in New Jersey. Kathryn, six months old, cooed softly in the back seat. We discussed what this meant—being closer to my family, moving to a new city, and taking on a fresh challenge. My mother's face lit up when we told her. Rita, ever adventurous, was all in.

The decision was made. Better compensation. Faster advancement. A job that checked the personal fulfillment box.

I told Peg first. She wasn't surprised. My meetings with Sandy, Tom, and John were harder. I fought back tears as we reflected on the past ten years of growth, learning, and friendship. Tom reminded me of how far back we went. We exchanged hugs and he said he was very sorry to see me leave.

Leaving Sixth and Sycamore was difficult. I sat in my car for a few minutes before turning the key. I reflected on leaving the place where I'd met my life partner, welcomed our daughter, and learned from mentors who shaped my career. P&G had given me the confidence to take on any challenge.

And I knew none of it would have happened without Peg's matchmaking instincts or Dr. Dave Wilemon's vision and guidance.

Grateful? Absolutely.

Ready for the next challenge? Without a doubt.

23

RESURRECTING POST CEREALS, THE OLDEST GENERAL FOODS BRAND

WHEN WE ARRIVED IN NEW YORK, RITA AND I WERE INVITED to a celebratory evening with Bill Korab and his wife. We had front-row orchestra seats at Lincoln Center for the revival of *Camelot*, starring Richard Burton, Christine Ebersole, and Richard Muenz. Burton was brilliant, Ebersole radiant, and Muenz's rendition of "If Ever I Would Leave You" brought the house down.

Dinner followed at La Côte Basque—one of New York's top Zagat-rated restaurants. It was a delightful way to start our New York journey and yet another indication that we were joining a considerate and gracious group of people. Although there was little business discussion, it was clear that Bill and I were excited to get started working together. The challenge of reviving another historic brand was invigorating. Post Cereals was created by C.W. Post in the late 1800s and was the brand that started what became General Foods.

The Post business had been "milked" with relatively low marketing spending, a lack of new product introductions and limited capital spending to help squeeze out as much profit and cash as possible. The issue of nutrition, which had become a serious negative, was also not being addressed. There was a lack of coordination with R&D.

On the following Thursday, eight of us departed from Westchester Airport at 6:30 a.m. and flew to Battle Creek, Michigan, home to our manufacturing facility and R&D Group. These organizations had not seen a brand management person in well over a year. We arrived back at Westchester at 10:45, just beating the 11 p.m. close of the airport.

On Friday, we spent the day refining our plans, incorporating input from Battle Creek, and meeting with all the brand groups to finalize plans. We worked until about 6:00 p.m., ignoring the 1:00 p.m. summer-hour departure time. While my objective was not to change the culture, I was nevertheless excited about what I saw as an enthusiastic response to the urgency that was developing.

The following week, we formally presented the plan to Bill Korab. I had kept Bill up to date on our progress, and he was supportive. By the end of next week, the plan, which included a hefty spending increase, was presented and approved by GF's top management. The following were the key components:

- **New Products**: Accelerated the development of new products. By the spring of 1982, we had introduced three new products: Fruit and Fiber, Smurfberry Crunch, and a Raisin Bran line extension.

- **Nutrition**: Analyzed the nutritional profiles of all brands. Created a sweetening system to lower sugar levels, reduced sodium levels, and optimized the blend of added vitamins and other nutritional ingredients.

- **Advertising:** Challenged Grey and Ogilvy agencies with creating breakthrough campaigns. Ed Meyer and David Ogilvy, the agency CEOs, were personally engaged.

- **Promotion**: Focused on providing better value and captured the interest of the grocery trade and the consumer.

- **Capital Spending**: Battle Creek installed equipment that generated attractive paybacks and facilitated the creation of unique new products.

- **Packaging**. A uniform Post design format was created to enhance consumer recognition.

An example of the nutrition challenge was Grape Nuts, our flagship brand, which contained over 3,000 mg of sodium per serving. We needed to reduce this very unhealthy level without degrading the eating enjoyment of our salt addicted consumers. We conducted a "blind test" in which consumers were asked to choose between two alternatives. While we expected the current product to prevail over a 400 mg sodium version, the 91 percent preference for the current product was stunning, back to the drawing board.

The solution came from the recognition that, over time, people adapt to what they eat. Every six months, we reduced the sodium level by 250 mg. Nobody, not even our heaviest users, noticed. Today, Grape Nuts is a very successful brand with only 280 mg of sodium. We made similar progress in sugar reduction.

The Breakfast Foods Division was executing its plan effectively. When CEO Jim Ferguson approached my office on a Friday morning in mid-July, I believed that we were about to take a bow for our efforts. Not the case. Jim had an issue, and the issue was with me.

The problem was that I was violating the 1:00 Friday afternoon summer hours. Almost all of the Breakfast Foods personnel were following me out the door from 5:00 to 6:00 p.m. on Friday. He reiterated the importance of employees striking a balance between work, family, and personal goals.

He volunteered a new personal goal for me: to learn how to play golf. Of the members of the executive staff, I stood virtually alone as a non-participant.

The solution was a 2:00 p.m. golf lesson at Winged Foot Golf Club on the next five Fridays. The lessons were set up with Tommy Neoporte, one of the country's premier golf instructors.

Tommy Neoporte— Head pro at Winged Foot Golf Club. Taught me how to play the game. A great guy and an outstanding teacher.

While I was a bit stunned, I agreed and began to develop not only great respect but also a genuine love for the game. Tommy thought I was a "natural," with good hand-eye coordination developed from basketball. My initial golf round was a very respectable 93 on the challenging Winged Foot course. I must confess that this score has decreased slightly over the years; 96 just doesn't sound as good. My exploits in golf will follow in a separate, totally honest chapter of its own.

While I was occupied with cereal, syrup, and golf, Rita was establishing a home base for our family. We bought a house in Purchase, New York, about ten minutes from the office. Purchase has a pleasant rural feel, with big-city shopping nearby in White Plains. The Big Apple was only a short train ride. My parents and the Village Deli's delicacies were only ninety minutes away, and Judy, Len, and baby Dina were about a two-hour drive.

24

ON PLAN, PROMOTION,
AND DMH IS BORN

THE PLAN WORKED. FOUR YEARS OF SHARE DETERIORATION WERE reversed, and Post Cereal's share increased from under 12 percent to 14 percent by the end of 1980. Log Cabin syrup had a record high share at year's end. The first quarter of 1981 was on track to exceed our revenue and profit objectives.

On March 28, 1981, two days before my thirty-fourth birthday, I was summoned to Phil Smith's office. Joining Phil were Jim Ferguson and Jim Tappan, who was the EVP responsible for the Breakfast Food Division. I was being promoted to division president, consistent with the commitment that was made when I joined GF. As Bill Dordelman predicted, GF's top management seemed to provide the support that I had from my P&G mentors.

The balance of 1981 and the subsequent years of 1982 and 1983 maintained the division's strong momentum. At the end of 1983, Post Cereals had a 17.5 percent share and was viewed as the industry's innovator. We introduced several new products, line extensions, and product improvements, significantly improved the nutritional profile of our brands, and continued to sharpen our marketing programs. Profitability was at an all-time high.

The division continued to benefit from the strong leadership of Chuck Marcy and Rick Powers. We recruited outstanding individuals such as Carl Harrington (Wharton MBA, President of IWMF), Steve Burke (Harvard MBA, CEO of Comcast), Karen King (Kellogg MBA, Kraft Director of Marketing), Cynthia Vahlkamp (MPA Princeton, EVP Starbucks), Laura McCorvie (NYU MBA, McCorvie and Partners Founder), Jane Drittell (Wharton), Donna Webster (Wharton MBA, VP at Stamford Health), and many others.

Over time, I adopted General Foods' more relaxed approach to the business. I spent more time with my family and even utilized summer hours to play golf on Friday afternoons. Jim Tappan was my boss. He was also ex-P&G and believed in and followed GF's "autonomous divisions" philosophy. He provided input and support when we needed it. He was an excellent golfer and helped me improve my game.

The Herskovits family enjoyed life in Purchase. Kathryn attended SUNY at Purchase Day School, where they created a special program for her. She became an expert in sign language and was able to communicate effectively with her deaf grandparents. As always, Rita had lots of friends and was elected president of the local chapter of the National Council of Jewish Women. Rita and Kathryn were globe-trotters—South Africa, Kenya, Europe, Brazil, and Israel among their stops.

Rita's parents and younger brothers, Kent and Andrew, were with us most of the summers. We regularly visited my parents and stocked up on the entrées I had helped create. They were still a featured product of the Village Deli and served as a satisfying dinner when Rita did not feel like cooking.

DMH

As 1982 came to a close, we learned Rita was pregnant. David Michael Herskovits was born on July 15, 1983. Unlike Kathryn, David was a sleeper—through the night from birth, plus long daytime naps. Around age two, he "woke up" and became highly active. Like most boys, he had his moments growing up, but he brought tremendous joy to everyone who knew him.

David was in the midst of achieving great things in alternative energy when we lost him unexpectedly to a heart attack in August 2021. The memorial that follows offers a fuller picture of the thirty-eight precious years we shared. As I think about these years, many events reflect his character, sensitivity, and appreciation for his origins. One such event stands out in my mind. In 2004, when he turned twenty-one, I offered to take him anywhere. I expected Las Vegas, Barcelona, Tahiti, or some other exotic destination.

Surprisingly, David chose Hungary. He wanted to see where I was born and raised and where his biological grandfather was buried. The trip was meaningful. It was an opportunity to discuss his future and my past. A few years earlier, Judy and Rita led a trip that found Andy's grave in a small town on the Austrian border called Radja. When we arrived, we met the mayor, who was fourteen years old when he heard about a handsome couple with two beautiful children who were caught trying to escape.

When we arrived, Radja was experiencing a major drought. There had not been any precipitation for over eight weeks. As we neared the makeshift cemetery, thunder roared and the skies opened up. We stood by Andy's grave, soaked to the bone but reveling in what seemed to be a sign from above. It was a moment I will never forget.

Not being able to witness David's continuing development as a person and as a businessman has been the greatest disappointment of my life. I do, however, have positive feelings from the DMH Foundation that Rita is championing. The Foundation is building on David's efforts to educate and inspire future generations to develop solutions to the environmental issues our planet is facing. Details of their efforts follow the Memorial to David.

25

Re-Evaluating Cereal Strategy

As 1983 was coming to an end, we celebrated the third consecutive year of very positive cereal and syrup results. Our management team gathered in a nearby conference center to formulate our strategies for 1984 and beyond. I had growing concerns:

- Much of our gains over the last three years were derived from developing and executing superior marketing programs. We believed that Kellogg's and General Mills were "sleeping at the switch," having cut marketing spending. Both companies assigned new cereal teams, and we expected them to be far more aggressive

- The Post Cereal business was at a significant cost of goods disadvantage versus Kellogg, which had invested heavily in automating its cereal processes. In the Fall of 1983, Kellogg raised its wage rates significantly. Post shared the same union, and they expected Post to meet Kellogg's wages. There was a reasonable chance that we were headed for a crippling strike.

- The new brand concepts we were working with were not judged to be as strong as those introduced over the last three years. We purchased a double extruder that promised the development of new and unique cereals. However, these new products were still twelve to eighteen months away. In the interim, we expected our competitors to be more aggressive in expanding new brands.

A Monumental Strategic Solution

The morning session ended with general agreement on the above issues. While the group went to lunch, I stayed behind and jotted notes that helped me refine the idea that was now dominating my brain. After lunch, I delivered what had become clear to me as the best strategic path:

BUY KELLOGG AND SELL POST

I wrote those five words on the whiteboard and let the group absorb the idea. Then, I laid out the rationale:

- Kellogg's has a dominant position in the cereal category. They are two and a half times the size of Post. They have not taken full advantage of this position. I believed that we would.

- Antitrust laws wouldn't allow us to own both Kellogg and Post, but we could sell Post quickly. Interested buyers would likely include Quaker, Unilever, Nestlé, Kraft, and Ralston Purina.

- Importantly, the Kellogg Foundation charter called for them to sell their 30 percent stake in the Kellogg company before the end of 1984. Acquiring these shares now would help ensure success in acquiring at least the controlling interest in the company.

- The transactions being proposed would set the stage for further General Foods acquisitions.

As I scanned the room, I sensed excitement about the idea. We agreed that I would lead the highly confidential project and work with the GF strategic planners to prepare the necessary documentation.

The General Foods Strategy Group was highly respected throughout the organization, including top management. They were very supportive of the "buy Kellogg" idea. We presented to Jim Tappan. He knew Bill Smithburg, the CEO of Quaker, and determined that Quaker would have a strong interest in purchasing Post. It is incredible what you can accomplish on a golf course.

We were now in motion on what I thought could be a transformative strategy for General Foods—one that would not only secure our future in cereal but also propel us into a position of leadership in the food industry.

Presentations to Smith and Ferguson

Phil Smith was the future leader of General Foods, and his approval was critical. From the start of our presentation, I had the sense that he would be a tough sell. I reviewed our concerns and emphasized that we were not willing to accept a strategy that failed to build on the momentum of the past three years.

One of Phil's concerns was financing—the current 9–10 percent interest rates resulted in financials that he viewed as borderline. He also questioned who would manage the business and how. Would I move to Battle Creek to run it? Without determining whether Rita, let alone Kathryn, could absorb yet another adventure, I responded that if it was best for the business, I would.

Phil summarized. He viewed the idea as solid strategic thinking. Although he had concerns, he agreed to support the proposal.

That next morning, Phil Smith and Jim Tappan joined me in Mr. Fergusson's office. I summarized what we were proposing and why we thought it made sense. Jim Tappan shared the positive feedback from Quaker's CEO. Phil agreed with the direction but reiterated his reservations.

Jim sat back and said nothing for a few seconds. He appeared to be in deep thought. He said that while he understood the merits of the proposal, there were things being considered by the Board that hindered moving quickly. He indicated that he was very pleased with the progress of the cereal business and that he felt 1984 would continue our strong performance. I chimed in with my concerns, but it did not alter his position.

Jim Tappan and Phil made gratuitous comments about revisiting the issue during the summer and got up and left. Jim asked me to stay. He said he wanted to make sure that I knew that he recognized and appreciated the positive impact I was having on the business and the organization. I thanked him, said I would do my best, and left.

I was disappointed and confused. Were there really competing priorities? How could we let this highly attractive opportunity pass us by? What about all the discussion about entrepreneurship and risk-taking? Are we actually setting ourselves up to be acquired? Rita and I went out to dinner and agreed to leave the business discussion for the upcoming weekend.

26

TIMING, MIKE MILES, AND A NEW OPPORTUNITY

TIMING CAN BE A CRITICAL FACTOR IN BOTH BUSINESS AND life decisions. And timing was undoubtedly at play that Saturday morning when I answered the phone.

"Hi, this is Mike Miles. My apologies for calling on a weekend, but this couldn't wait."

"Not a problem, Mike—it's been a long time," I replied.

Mike and I knew each other from my days at P&G. He had been with Leo Burnett in Chicago, Bold's advertising agency. I had followed his career, including his successful tenure at Kentucky Fried Chicken (KFC), where he rebuilt relationships with franchisees and the legendary Colonel Sanders himself. Now, as the new CEO of Kraft, he was already making waves, but he was just getting started.

> *Mike Miles was a pragmatic, no-nonsense leader. After ten years at Leo Burnett, he joined KFC and turned the struggling business around. As CEO of Kraft, he produced significant growth, leading to Philip Morris's purchase of Kraft in 1989.*

Mike was direct and to the point: *"I hired recruiters to identify three or four of the top young talents in the*

industry—leaders who have proven themselves in energizing neglected busi-
nesses. I believe that with the right people, we can make Kraft the dominant
food company."

He explained that I was one of the four individuals identified. He was well aware of my accomplishments at P&G and General Foods and said the position he was about to describe was tailor-made for me.

The Opportunity at Kraft

The role: CEO of The Kraft Dairy Group, a $1 billion autonomous division based in Philadelphia, managing over thirty-five plants, six thousand people, and well-known brands like Breyers, Sealtest, Breakstone, and Light n' Lively.

Unlike at GF, where there are two levels between the General Managers and the CEO, and they are down the hall, I would be reporting to a CEO in Chicago with double-digit direct reports—assurance of autonomy if the company performs.

It was a compelling opportunity. And the timing couldn't have been more serendipitous. Any other Saturday morning during my four years at General Foods, I would've reflexively used my old P&G line: I'm happy where I am, with the people I work with, and I'm not looking.

But this Saturday morning came on the heels of my disappointment over the Kellogg proposal being tabled. Mike's call found me at the height of my frustration.

Mike told me that John Tucker, Kraft's VP of Human Resources, would call Monday with the details. He encouraged me to take the weekend to think and not respond until I had the full picture.

John Tucker was more than just a capable HR executive—he was Mike Miles's "right hand," operating almost as co-CEO. He was instrumental in attracting the young talent that drove Kraft's impressive growth in the decade that followed. More than a dozen Kraft alums from that era would go on to lead billion-dollar companies. John and I have remained good friends.

By the time John called on Monday, Rita and I had already talked it through. Assuming the compensation was appropriate, it was too good to pass up. As Mike said, this was another chance to turn around a storied business, and it represented a substantial increase in scope and responsibility.

I was familiar with Philadelphia from my courtship at Penn, and my sister Judy was a few minutes away across the river in New Jersey.

Perhaps the most significant factor in my decision was my growing unease about the Post business. I couldn't shake the feeling that Kellogg was about to "wake up." Given their structural advantages, we'd have a hard time keeping pace. I did not have a clear vision of where I wanted to get to and how I would get there.

27

THE DAIRY GROUP TURNAROUND; JUDGE JUDY & FAMILY

BEFORE I KNEW IT, I WAS IN THE MIDDLE OF ANOTHER adventure. The transition from GF to Kraft Dairy Group was easier than my departure from P&G. While I had great admiration for many at General Foods, I hadn't built the same deep personal bonds. I still held the organization in high regard and remained friends with Bill Dordelman and Bill Korab, among others.

For 1984, The Kraft Dairy Group projected revenues over $1 billion but a loss approaching $20 million—unacceptable performance that would require some significant changes.

Settling in Philadelphia

Before tackling the business issues, let me report on the family side of the move. As usual, Rita was responsive to the challenges of finding a place to live, schools, doctors, a temple, and a host of other services. She found an incredible house in Gladwyne, Pennsylvania, that deserves mention.

The house was built by a builder on eight glorious acres just above the Schuylkill River, about ten miles north of downtown. The house was

14,000 square feet with varying levels for the different spaces. It was an architectural masterpiece.

We loved the house, but it was priced well above what we considered our "maximum." The house was being sold by the sister of the owner, who had passed away from a heart attack, trudging up the roughly three hundred-foot elevation the house sat on. He was an African American doctor renowned for his philanthropy. He treated the homeless and never took money from people who could not afford it. In his will, he specified criteria for someone to qualify to purchase the property. Two different parties who made offers were flatly refused, not for price but for some other reason designated by the doctor.

His sister, who was head of the Dallas public education system, oversaw the sale of the property. She was a lovely person, and she fell in love with the two youngsters, ages five and one, that Rita dragged up the hill. Our family was the first to meet all the required qualifications for the house. The sister accepted our "maximum" offer. At the closing for an additional $2,000, she gave us a $50,000 Mason Hamlin piano so Kathryn could continue her lessons and about $20,000 worth of furniture.

A great feature of the house was a bedroom apartment just beyond the kitchen. As school started in 1984, Andrew, Rita's younger brother, moved in. Andrew was an incredibly bright, interesting youngster. It was clear that he would not receive the kind of education he deserved at the high school he was scheduled to attend.

The Harriton School is one of the top high schools in the country, and with Andrew living at our Gladwyne abode, he qualified to attend. He performed brilliantly, including being elected President of the senior class after only two years attending this prestigious academic institution. Andrew became our third child, and we probably could not have operated all the gadgets and appliances had it not been for his mechanical aptitude.

Andrew attended the Wharton School at Penn. As will be discussed later, he participated in companies that I later became involved in. Andrew's daughter Grace was born in 2009 and has been a source of exceptional joy for us. Andrew married Kelly Geary in 2017, and her two children, Gigi and Cash, have become valued members of our family. Today, Andrew is CEO of a major education company.

Kent, 17 years younger than Rita, also had an active role in our family. We bonded over sports, often spending hours discussing teams and games. Kent and his wife, Michelle, both Miami of Ohio grads, have four very talented children. Kent is the manager of the Cincinnati division of Halo's Promotional Products.

A Wake-Up Call for the Dairy Group

While the family settled easily into its new environment, dealing with the Kraft Dairy Group business was more complex and challenging. The one saving grace: the team was top-notch. It included some of the GF associates who followed me to Philadelphia. Unlike some of the other challenging situations I faced, the Dairy Group was well-staffed with highly competent people.

Bob Creighton was the marketing manager. Bob was an experienced and capable manager. I was thrilled to find that one of my favorite people at P&G, Bob Baker, was running the ice cream business. Bob graduated with an MBA from Columbia and is one of the most talented marketing people I have come across in my career. We remain good friends.

We hired another P&G alumnus, Mitch Weinick. Mitch was a no-nonsense leader who consistently delivered outstanding results. He, too, remains a close friend. Chuck Marcy, my top lieutenant in the cereal business, joined us a few months later.

Throughout my business life, I have been blessed by having outstanding administrative assistants. Marian Hartnett was no exception. She was personable, smart, and very organized—the perfect assistant.

Bob Baker, Mitch Weinick, and Chuck Marcy, three outstanding executives and good friends, the foundation of the teams that produced recoveries at GF and Kraft and later at Specialty Foods.

With a solid organization in place, we moved quickly on priorities:

Selling the Milk Business—The milk business, which accounted for about a third of the company's revenue, was largely responsible for the lack of profitability. Our analysis of the milk industry was clear—this was not an attractive long-term business.

In our first nine months, we sold all twelve milk operations, generating cash while disposing of money-losing assets. The approach that began with the purchase of the Record Runner distributor worked well in selling the milk assets. We determined a fair price and did not sell unless that price was met.

Expanding Breyers Ice Cream and Yogurt—Breyers ice cream was the leading US brand despite being marketed only east of the Mississippi. Over the next eighteen months, aided by the acquisition of Knudson on the West Coast, we achieved national distribution and enhanced the profitability of the brand. Breyers yogurt was also expanded, building on the ice cream's successful footprint.

A new Breyers ice cream package design was created by the company's amateur package designer. While some questioned the use of black on an ice cream package, analysis showed that the impactful new package was responsible for about a 10 percent increase in 1985 Breyers revenue. The basic black design continues today, forty years later.

Restaging Sealtest and Breakstone—The Sealtest and Breakstone brands were restaged behind improved products, updated packaging designs, and new marketing plans, including improved advertising.

Light n' Lively Nutrition Improved—Light n' Lively ice milk and yogurt were reformulated to provide better nutrition.

1984 ended on a high note, as the Dairy Group exceeded its revenue and profit targets. In 1985, the Dairy Group generated a $20 million profit—a $40 million improvement versus the previous year. Mike Miles held to his promise of a truly autonomous division. Most decisions were made without leaving Philadelphia.

In late 1985, Mike and John Tucker joined us in the ribbon-cutting ceremony of a shiny new downtown headquarters for the company. I was on the board of trustees of the Philadelphia College of Pharmacy, and we donated the valuable land on which our previous offices stood to the college.

At the headquarters opening, we celebrated a year of significant accomplishments. Also joining us were Philadelphia Mayor Goode and Chief of Police Kevin Tucker—John's twin brother.

Kevin was previously a Secret Service agent who, as the chief of police, was responsible for cleaning up the historically corrupt Philadelphia Police Department. Shortly after our ceremony, he was diagnosed with brain cancer and was not given much chance for survival. He participated in a clinical trial but was part of the group that did not receive medical intervention. Kevin was with us another twenty years, probably a result of very effective prayers by his sweet mother, who appeared to have a special connection upstairs. The Tuckers were good friends, and John and his family remain among our favorites.

Judge Judy and Our Family

On September 5, 1985, my sister Judith Herskovits Wizmur was sworn in as a United States bankruptcy judge. The ceremony was moving, with our mother, brother Mark, and me in attendance. Tears flowed as Judy reflected on her journey and those who supported her. At the time, she was believed to be the youngest bankruptcy judge ever appointed.

Amazing—my baby sister became a federal judge. The dreams of the grandfather she never knew far surpassed. What a country, and what a sister.

Judy continues to live in Mount Laurel, NJ, and has been married to Leonard for 53 years. She retired from the bench in 2021. Her daughter Dina is an attorney, has three wonderful children, and is married to a very successful fund manager and all-around great guy, Ted Gleser.

The Wizmur's son Matthew, my godson, was born on March 30th, 1984. Matthew's arrival on my birthday doubled his welcome gift. Matthew is married to Rochelle, a speech therapist. They have two talented girls, Natalie and Ilana. Matt is the last of the four Wizmurs to attend Rutgers Law School.

Family get-togethers, which occur frequently, also include my brother Mark and his lovely wife, Joanie, and the families of their daughters, Ariel and Jessica. Mark retired from a successful insurance career. It is pretty remarkable that "The Kid" has three grandkids.

And then there's my daughter Kathryn, who has been dazzling everyone at family gatherings for the last forty-six years. Last we left her, she was determined to be a genius by child development experts at Columbia University. She excelled at the Baldwin School in Philadelphia and Lake Forest Academy.

She was accepted at the best colleges, including Rita's dream school, Wellesley, but to our surprise, she enrolled in what we thought was her "safe school," the Stern School of Business at NYU. She was, is, and always will be a New Yorker, and she needed business to afford her liberal arts lifestyle.

Today, Kathryn and her "significant other," Troy, live in Brooklyn and travel the world. She is a partner and COO of the *What If Media Group,* which has grown to over 125 people. I not only love her dearly, but I also have the utmost respect for the independent, competent, and caring person she has become.

Completing the family circle, both my parents lived until the age of ninety-three, my father passing away in 2013 and my mother in 2018. Their final fifty years were marked by pride as they watched their children, grandchildren, and great-grandchildren flourish. It's incredible to think that one brave woman thrown from a train in Hungary became the matriarch of such a vibrant legacy.

28

Purchase of Frusen Glädjé and Knudsen & Polar Bar Problem

1985 was an outstanding year for the Kraft Dairy Group. Among the many drivers of our performance were two acquisitions: Frusen Glädjé ice cream and the Knudsen Dairy Company. Neither deal followed the typical playbook for food industry acquisitions, and both proved to be highly successful.

The Commercial that Spurred the Purchase of Frusen Glädjé

The Frusen Glädjé story begins in the 1970s when a Polish immigrant named Reuben Mattus set out to create the best ice cream in the world. He used high butterfat content and premium ingredients. He packaged his ice cream in distinctive cylindrical pints and gave it a made-up Scandinavian-sounding name: Häagen-Dazs.

Though it started slowly, Häagen-Dazs gained traction and distribution, launching the super-premium ice cream category.

Richard Smith, a New York entrepreneur, took notice. He launched his own super-premium ice cream brand, Frusen Glädjé, mimicking the Nordic naming convention.

By 1985, the super-premium segment was rapidly growing. As the leader in the ice cream market, we couldn't ignore it. The question became: should we create a new brand or acquire one of the two existing players?

I posed the question to my friend Marvin Honig, previously co-conspirator on Gain, now creative director at DDB. Marvin wasn't just a creative talent—he had excellent strategic instincts. I explained the market situation, and Marvin promised to think it over.

A week later, he showed up at my Philadelphia office, unannounced. He walked to the whiteboard and wrote, in bold letters:

BUY FRUSEN GLÄDJÉ, RUN THIS AD

He then showed an actual demo tape of a 30-second Frusen Glädjé commercial in which his secretary played the role. It had the brilliant simplicity that was the trademark of Marvin's creative work.

30-Second Frusen Glädjé Commercial

Announcer: *If you don't feel guilty, it wasn't that good.*

Woman: *I ate all the Frusen Glädjé*

Husband: *You ate all the what?*

Woman: *I ate all the Frusen Glädjé!*

Announcer: *Frusen Glädjé, the ice cream under the dome. So creamy, so delicious, so rewarding.*

Woman defiantly: *And I'd do it again...*

Announcer: *Enjoy the Guilt. Frusen Glädjé.*

I loved the commercial and agreed with Marvin's conclusion to buy Frusen Glädjé. Buying a company based on an ad that hadn't even aired was highly unorthodox, but it was the right move.

Richie Smith, the owner of Frusen Glädjé, and I met, and I put an offer on the table. Richie knew of our milk plant sales and understood that our offer was fair and not negotiable. We shook hands, and thirty days later, we owned Frusen Glädjé, and Richard Smith was a rich man.

By the time we closed the transaction, the new commercial was already filmed. The casting was brilliant. The commercial catapulted the career of the young actress who ate all the Frusen Glädjé. We began airing the commercial, and the business took off almost immediately. In its first year, the brand recorded more than a 50 percent increase in revenue.

The Honor and Satisfaction of the Effies Followed by Disappointment

The Effie Award celebrates advertising that delivers outstanding business results. This prestigious award is presented at a black tie gala in New York City. Our Frusen Glädjé commercial won a gold medal. Attending were DDB founder Bill Bernbach, Creative Director Marvin Honig, Mike Miles, and I.

The gala was on March 30, 1987—my fortieth birthday and my parents' anniversary. My family was disappointed that they couldn't celebrate this important day with me. But this was a secondary issue.

The main issue: On the same day, March 30th, at the Louisiana SuperDome in New Orleans at 9:10 p.m., the ball was being tipped off to determine the NCAA national basketball champion. It had been twenty-two grueling years that I agonized over every dribble, every turnover, foul shot, basket, and rebound of Syracuse basketball. They were now in the championship game. And where was I?

I was sitting at the head table of the Effies, with three titans of the consumer goods industry, quite a distance from the orphanage by the lake and the bombed-out streets of Budapest. While I appreciated the significance of those facts, my eyes kept drifting to my watch. I calculated at 7:10, after cocktail hour was over, and we were now seated, that we had sixteen awards to go. At eight minutes each, we should be done before 9:30. A half hour to taxi back to the Helmsley Palace, where I can watch the second half.

To my chagrin, the first two awards averaged twelve minutes each. I did the quick math: 12 x 16 = 192 minutes, over three hours—I miss the game completely. Surprisingly, the award for Frusen Glädjé was the third presented, well before our next-to-last position shown on the program. They showed the Frusen Glädjé ad, told the story about how it was developed, and the results it generated. Mr. Bernbach and Mike Miles were introduced, and Marvin and I were called up to accept the award. I was honored to accept in front of this august group and tried hard to dismiss the thoughts of basketball from my mind. A glance at my watch; another thirteen minutes had gone by.

I got back to my seat, positioned the Effie award on the table, and was about to sit when Mike stopped me. *"You are dismissed, Mr. Herskovits,"* he said. *"There is a limo downstairs that will take you back to your hotel, and you will not miss a minute of the game. Happy Birthday!"* Bill and Marvin also had best wishes for my birthday and the game.

Thank you very much, Mike!!!

I flew downstairs, into the limo, and was in my room before 9:00. On the desk was a birthday cake with "Happy 40th; Go Cuse" and a small bottle of champagne. I had told Mike about my dilemma, and I believe he orchestrated all the events. To this day, I remain stunned that he was able to change the order of the Effie awards so I could see a basketball game.

Now, did the game really matter that much? You bet it did. It was Bobby Knight's Indiana Hoosiers against Jim Boeheim's Syracuse Orangemen. The two Hall of Fame coaches received even more media attention than the players. It was a great game, two excellent teams playing their hearts out. And...it appeared that the Cuse was going to prevail. They were leading by a point with five seconds to go, and Indiana's guard seemed stuck at half court. He escaped the Cuse press, whipped the ball to the left corner to their other guard, Kieth Smart. He elevated on his patented jump shot, and a second later, with no time left on the clock, the ball is through the net for a one-point Indiana victory.

A true heartbreaker. I sipped the remaining champagne and fell into bed with a bevy of mixed emotions. What a night.

Knudsen Purchased Out of Bankruptcy

Although Knudsen did not win any awards, the acquisition was highly successful. The company was founded in 1919 by Danish immigrants Carl and Tom Knudsen and grew to become the leading dairy on the West Coast. In 1983, it was sold to Winn Enterprises. They acquired Foremost Dairies and a dairy in Kansas. The rapid pace of expansion led to significant financial stress, operational issues, and union strife to the point that by September 1986, Knudsen filed for Chapter 11 bankruptcy protection and was put up for sale.

A key challenge for potential buyers was the labor restriction that prevented spinning off the milk business. The only way to lift this major burden was to sell it to someone who would honor the commitments that had been made. Our analysis indicated that Hughes Markets was the only viable buyer.

I had developed a strong relationship with their CEO, Fred McLaren, and Hughes contracted to buy the milk business only from us. Dreyers, the leading ice cream brand on the West Coast, appeared to be the only other bidder. They coveted Knudsen's ice cream business and the opportunity to broaden their product line. We hired one of the country's top bankruptcy attorneys, Ron Trost of Sidley & Austin, on my sister's recommendation, to represent us.

Mike Miles was adamant about winning the bid. Knudsen could be a highly profitable asset and would strengthen Kraft's position on the West Coast. He strongly suggested that we bid $80 million—a number we were certain Dreyers could not match. He

Ron Trost- A great lawyer and a delightful person. Instrumental in the successful Knudsen acquisition.

remarked, only half-jokingly, "If you don't make the winning bid, you might not want to come home."

Ron and I were convinced that Dreyers would not even bid. While I was certainly concerned about Mike's directive, I was inclined to bid the minimum $40 million amount set by the court in consultation with creditors.

The night before the court session, I had an epiphany. We prepared two offers, one for $40 million and one for $80 million. Ron had one in each pocket, and he would wait for Dreyers to show their hand first.

The next day, the judge entered the courtroom and got right to the point. He asked all with bids to come forward. As expected, Ron and the attorney for Dreyers' were the only ones approaching the bench. For what seemed like an eternity, the two attorneys just stood there looking at each other. The judge repeated himself, *"Gentlemen, your bids please."* Ron fumbled through his pockets, continuing his Academy Award-deserving performance. The judge turned to the Dreyers' attorney, and he was forced to act.

"We would like a continuance, your honor, given that Kraft has unfairly contracted to sell the milk business to the only viable purchaser, Hughes Markets," he argued.

The judge quickly dismissed the argument. Ron went into his left pocket and produced the lower bid, thereby saving Kraft $40 million.

We savored our victory at Wolfgang Puck's Chinois in Santa Monica, one of the finest restaurants in the Los Angeles area. Mike Miles happily agreed to fund the expensive celebration.

Knudsen significantly outperformed our acquisition targets in 1986 and beyond and was instrumental in achieving West Coast distribution on a number of our brands, including Breyers ice cream.

As we were completing the first half of 1986, the Dairy Group was trending well ahead of plan with major contributions from the two very successful acquisitions. Rita and I planned an Independence Day barbecue for the executive staff and their families.

Listeria and Polar Bars

The Fourth of July barbecue never happened. On July 3rd, just as I was leaving the office, the phone rang. It was Mike Miles. The Food and Drug Administration (FDA) had just informed Kraft that our Polar Bar product had been linked to a serious outbreak of listeria, which was, at the time, a little-known but dangerous bacterial contaminant. Six people in the Richmond, Virginia area had become seriously ill, and Polar Bars appeared to be the common denominator.

A Kraft plane was en route to Philadelphia. By seven that evening, I was in a conference room at Kraft headquarters in Glenview, Illinois. Over the next thirty-six hours, Mike and I, along with leaders from research, manufacturing, and public relations, immersed ourselves in learning about listeria and developing a response plan.

At 5 a.m. on July 5th, we submitted a detailed plan to the FDA that included:

1. A total recall of all Polar Bar products. Ultimately, Polar Bar was discontinued.

2. Shutting down the Richmond manufacturing facility.

3. Implementing rigorous inspections across all Kraft dairy facilities.

4. Launching a comprehensive "Total Quality" initiative to upgrade our systems and facilities to ensure safety on every front.

These measures went beyond the FDA's requirements, and they came at a steep financial cost, but Kraft's reputation and consumer trust were far more critical.

In the last half of 1986, the focus was on our manufacturing facilities. Our "Total Quality" task force visited every plant at least once a month. Our people responded to the challenge, and we passed all of our internal and FDA inspections. Despite a very strong first half of the year, including two successful acquisitions, the Dairy Group missed its 1986 revenue and profit targets. While this was a challenging period, it was one of significant learning, and the manufacturing improvements not only ensured safety but also created substantial long-term efficiencies.

Over the next two and a half years, the Dairy Group delivered outstanding performance, consistently exceeding revenue and profit expectations. As we approached the July 4th holiday in 1988, two years to the day since the listeria call, I was once again summoned to Chicago.

Mike Miles and John Tucker had news: I was being promoted to president of the newly formed Kraft Dairy and Frozen Products Group (KD&F), which would include all of Kraft's frozen brands—Lender's, Tombstone, Budget Gourmet—as well as the Dairy Group. Having played a role in the acquisition of each of those companies, I was familiar with their potential and eager to take on the expanded challenge. Chuck Marcy, who followed me to Kraft from General Foods, would become president of the Dairy Group.

In addition, I would now lead Kraft's Total Quality initiative across the entire corporation, an effort that had started as a crisis response and was now being institutionalized company-wide.

And one more thing: I would be relocating to Kraft's Glenview headquarters in the Chicago suburb with an office right next to Mike Miles. Tucker gave me a knowing smile and said, *"Off the record,"* that I should view this move and my office location positively.

29

A Promotion, Chicago, Phillip Morris, Boca, and the Harvard Nutrition Roundtable

THE NEWS OF YET ANOTHER MOVE WAS NOT WELL-RECEIVED in Gladwyne, Pennsylvania. The Herskovits family had become firmly rooted. We were living in a beautiful home, surrounded by family—my sister was nearby, as were my parents. The schools that Kathryn and David attended were excellent. Rita, as always, had built a network of close friends and once again had a leadership role in the community.

We gave serious thought to staying in Philadelphia, which would have meant parting ways with Kraft and seeking a new opportunity. That choice was weighed against a major promotion—a substantial step forward in my career and our financial security. I liked and respected the outstanding Kraft executive team and was confident that the businesses being combined would be successful.

Ultimately, ambition and greed prevailed. We were moving to Chicago.

As she had done many times before, Rita stepped up to the challenge of relocating our lives. She quickly locked in top-tier schools, healthcare providers, services, and, of course, a new home.

Our next residence was another architectural gem, this time perched on a hill with a breathtaking view of Lake Michigan, in the North Shore suburb of Highland Park. The house was constructed almost entirely from granite. The original owner had purchased a granite quarry in Wisconsin and brought in two expert stonecutters from Venice, Italy, to craft each piece by hand. It took nine years to build. By the time it was finished, his kids were off to college, and his wife no longer wanted to leave their downtown Chicago home. It was sad to see the almost-empty closet the owner apparently used on his rare visits to the house. This beautiful piece of architecture was now ten years in the making and had never been lived in.

Like our experience in Gladwyne, this seller was particular. He wanted the right people to inhabit the masterpiece he had created. The realtor warned us that the owner had walked out of a closing after the buyers expressed something negative about the house.

This is where my architecture background came in handy. I offered sincere, specific praise for both the home's design and its construction. It was precisely what the seller wanted to hear. I even shared my philosophy on acquisitions: make a fair offer and stand by it. He accepted the bid. A few weeks later, we moved in.

Predictably, I was called away on a last-minute business trip, leaving Rita to handle the move yet again. I suspected, rightly, that this might be the last time I'd be able to get away with that well-worn routine. Still, Rita managed it all with her usual grace and efficiency.

The new environment in Chicago sparked a sense of exploration and excitement, at least for most of us. The one exception was Kathryn. She struggled with the school and the broader adjustment. Nothing seemed to compare to the world she had left behind. I am still unsure that she has forgiven me for uprooting her from her beloved East Coast.

Getting Settled in Kraft's Glenview Headquarters

I must admit I felt some apprehension as I walked into Kraft's Glenview headquarters on my first day. It reminded me of my arrival at P&G nearly two decades earlier, except this time, there was no Howard Morgens in the elevator offering encouragement, and I wasn't heading into a bullpen. I was stepping into a plush executive office directly next to Kraft's CEO.

I arrived early and poked my head into Mike Miles's office. To my surprise, he was already at his desk, hard at work. I wasn't sure whether I was trying to impress him by being early, or whether he was doing the same. We exchanged pleasantries, and I moved next door to my new office. Mike was not much for small talk outside of business.

As I sat behind my plush desk for the first time, I felt a strange emptiness. I was now president of a multibillion-dollar business. Yet, I didn't have a single direct report within a thousand miles aside from my new secretary, who arrived precisely one minute before the nine o'clock start time.

Fortunately, those feelings didn't last long. I began assembling a first-class leadership team, starting with the presidents of each of our four business units:

- **Chuck Marcy**: Dairy

- **Ernie Townsend**: Budget Gourmet

- **John Craig**: Lender's Bagels

- **Keith Reinhardt**: Tombstone Pizza

The other staff members were the "cream of the crop" in their respective functions. John Tucker and I meticulously selected individuals who were not only talented in their fields but also well-suited to work across our four business units. They included stars like Ellis Reynolds of Sales, Attorney Kathy Spear, Danny Strickland of R&D, Dave Weich of information systems, and Steve Poente of HR.

While this was a relatively lean executive group for a $4 billion business, I had complete confidence in our ability to make dramatic progress.

Our first order of business was an executive retreat in Scottsdale, Arizona. Over the course of three days, we conducted reviews of each business. It was a very productive meeting. We returned to Chicago aligned, motivated, and excited about what we could accomplish.

Phillip Morris Comes Calling

At about 5 p.m. on October 17, 1988, only a few months after I first arrived at Kraft headquarters and a month after our Arizona meeting, John Tucker called, "*Mike wants everybody in the boardroom at 7 p.m.— it's important.*"

In the conference room were all the division heads, John Tucker, our chief counsel, two outside lawyers, an investment banker, and, of course, Mike Miles.

"*Philip Morris has made an offer to purchase Kraft for ninety dollars a share,*" Mike announced. He then read the letter from Hamish Maxwell, Chair and CEO of Philip Morris, which detailed the offer. This was not totally unexpected. Jim Kilts, who followed me to Kraft from GF, and I heard the scuttlebutt that Philip Morris's acquisition of General Foods over a year before did not meet Philip Morris's expectations. It was the consensus that Philip Morris was looking to Kraft not only to continue its diversification but also to help it manage the food business.

The next few weeks were a blur of high-intensity activity. Our goal was to block the takeover if possible or, at the very least, drive up the price.

One major tactic: divesting parts of the company. The dairy business was the leading candidate. We visited entities judged capable and interested. Bain & Company in Boston had the resources and had the most interest. They were rapidly completing their due diligence, and we were close to determining a fair price.

While our efforts to keep Kraft independent were unsuccessful, we succeeded in raising the price to $113 per share, resulting in a total purchase price of $12,662,989,490. John Richman and Mike Miles led the sale price negotiations while John Tucker negotiated all the other details. The lifetime health care benefit that John obtained has been of great value to the Kraft executive group.

Kraft management signed three-year contracts that avoided the mass exodus that occurred at General Foods.

Over the next few days, the division heads met and committed to two goals: maintain Kraft's strong momentum and reverse General Foods' sharp decline. We wanted to produce such outstanding results that Mike Miles could compete to be the next CEO of Philip Morris. Given the company's deeply ingrained tobacco culture, this was a lofty goal. If we were successful, Mike would be the first non-smoking CEO in Philip Morris's history.

We had the team to pull it off. The division presidents were young, talented, and refreshingly non-political. Over the next two years, we far exceeded our objectives, almost doubling the food business's profits. My KD&F group made a significant contribution to this effort, increasing revenue by about 25 percent and more than doubling profits. The Breyers national expansion continued to be successful; our cultured, Lender's, and Budget Gourmet businesses were well ahead of plan, and Tombstone Pizza revenue more than doubled.

First Presence in Boca Raton

During the post-Philip Morris takeover period, there were a couple of important events that impacted our family and my career. In late 1989, we bought our first Boca Raton residence—a comfortable three-bedroom house in the golf community of Stonebridge. It served as a great weekend and holiday escape from the Windy City's freezing winter temperatures.

A couple of years later, we sold our house and moved to the Addison Condominiums on the beach in Boca, just south of the Boca Beach Club. The Addison is a fabulous building, and our five-bedroom double apartment served as a gathering place for our family. As usual, Rita made instant friends. A significant portion of our time was spent with Sandi and Kenny Greenblatt, multi-Tony-winning Broadway producers who were leaders of the social scene at the Addison. They have remained close friends for thirty-five years. Today, we enjoy watching their granddaughter, Adrianna Greenblatt, build her fast-rising movie career.

The Harvard Nutrition Roundtable (HNR)

In the fall of 1990, Holly Hayes, Kraft's brilliant strategy coordinator, nominated me to the HNR. The Roundtable is comprised of approximately forty members from around the world, who are highly influential in addressing nutritional issues. They manage the extensive Nurses' Study, which tracks nurses' diets and monthly blood profiles, with over three hundred thousand participants by the 2020s. HNR was the driving force in the elimination of trans fats in the United States.

The head of HNR has been Walter Willett, widely regarded as one of the world's leading nutrition experts. Walter is a remarkable man. At eighty years of age, he still rides his bicycle to work. It has been an absolute honor and pleasure to serve on HNR with Walter for some of the last thirty-five years as the only representative of large food manufacturers.

Knowing and interacting with giants like Walter has been one of the great benefits of my business career. Rita and I have met and, in many cases, gotten to know four US presidents, Margeret Thatcher, the king of Jordan, John Glenn, Bill Bradley, Tom Ridge, Harry Reid, agency heads Peter Georgescu, David Ogilvy, Leo Burnett and Ed Meyer, golfers Arnold Palmer, Payne Stewart, and Gary Player, among many others, five Nobel Prize winners, and numerous others who have made major contributions to our world. For an immigrant from Budapest and the daughter of deaf parents from Hamilton, Ohio, these encounters have been deeply humbling and a testament to the limitless opportunities our great country offers.

Mike Miles, CEO of Philip Morris

In August 1991, Kraft's division managers achieved their long-shot objective. The Philip Morris directors elected Mike Miles as CEO. Despite Mike's ascendency, three of the division presidents, Jim Kilts, Miles Marsh, and I, had informed management that we would not be staying beyond our three-year contracts. Dick Meyer, who worked at Leo Burnett with Mike, was appointed CEO of the food business.

About three months before the end of my three-year commitment to Phillip Morris, Dick asked to see me. The company was going to sell the Frozen business. Frozen did not fit Kraft's long-term vision of dry and refrigerated distribution systems. My services were no longer needed beyond a thirty-day transition period.

I was initially stunned, ignoring the fact that my imminent departure was approaching. Without saying a word, I recounted my accomplishments during my tenure at Kraft. I significantly exceeded my plan in five of my six years with Kraft (the only exception was the Polar Bar issue year), made three very successful acquisitions, and built solid organizations throughout the division. How could my services no longer be needed?

Then it dawned on me: the severance package I was receiving was meaningfully better than if I had finished my contract. Was a friend engineering a softer landing? John Tucker never confirmed it, but the package was indeed generous.

On June 8, 1992, I walked out of Kraft headquarters for the last time. Philip Morris later spun off the food business, eventually splitting Kraft into two companies. In 2008, Heinz acquired the Kraft food business.

30

RETIREMENT AND ICE CREAM

WHAT A POSITION TO BE IN: FORTY-FIVE YEARS OLD, FINANCIALLY independent, with a fabulous wife, two great kids, a beautiful home on Lake Michigan, and no job commitment.

So... now what? Retirement?

We decided to give it a try. Rita was delighted. She gladly handed over many of her logistic responsibilities. My days quickly settled into a routine: take David to school, pick him up, shuttle him to one of the seven sports he played, check the stock market, have dinner, maybe hit a few golf balls into the lake, watch TV, and call it a night. Repeat five times a week.

One ritual broke that monotony—Friday evening services at Temple B'nai Shalom in Skokie, Illinois, the only synagogue in the United States serving the deaf community. Led by the inspiring Rabbi Douglas Goldhamer, it had been a tremendous discovery for Rita's deaf parents. We quickly became deeply involved.

The temple began in a small storefront; we bought the store next door and donated it to expand its capacity. Kathryn donated all her Bat Mitzvah gift money to build a library, which is still known today as the Kathryn Elizabeth Herskovits Library. David used his presents to fund the Rabbi's trip to England and Scotland. Rita and I were extremely proud of our kids—not only in their outstanding performances at these momentous occasions, but also in their heartfelt generosity.

Despite the meaning we found at the temple, retirement didn't suit me. The decision not to retire was easy. But now what?

Over the next few weeks, I wrestled with the possibilities. Did I want to run a big company again? Go entrepreneurial? Was there anything on my business opportunities list worth pursuing?

The bigger question: Why? What was motivating me now?

It wasn't money or power, the usual drivers for people in my position. Was I still chasing the dreams of my biological father and of Béla to succeed in America? Was I trying to honor my father's legacy as an entrepreneur, a man whose exploits were legendary among his friends? Or was it something I'd learned from my stepfather, Nathan—how to persevere through adversity?

While I could not come up with a definitive answer about my motivation, I concluded that whatever came next had to be challenging, interesting, and involve people I truly enjoyed working with.

Two friendships from my Kraft days soon opened doors. Gary Greenberg invited me to join the board of Sage Inc., a company providing meals and supplies to airlines. Kraft had once acquired Sage and later sold it back to Gary and his partner.

Then there was Lou Weisbach, founder and CEO of HALO, a supplier of promotional products to several of my Kraft businesses. Lou's vision was bigger: expand into marketing consulting, strategic planning, package design, and logistics. My background was a perfect fit.

We agreed that I would buy 15 percent of the company and join him as a partner. Contracts were signed. Then, a major investment bank offered to take HALO public at a much higher valuation. I convinced Lou to void our contract and proceed with the IPO. I then agreed to join his board of directors.

HALO grew rapidly, approaching $1 billion in revenue, until some poor bets during the late '90s internet bubble stalled the momentum. The company later reorganized and emerged as a successful private company run by Marc

Simon, HALO's former chief legal counsel. My son David once blocked for Mark's son Danny in Giants football, and our families remain close.

Ice Cream for Sale

While these board roles were engaging, they didn't scratch the itch to be fully committed to something. That changed in early 1993.

Over lunch, Bob Morrison, the new CEO of Kraft General Foods, vented about the ice cream division's poor performance. The team that had built it was long gone. The company wanted to sell the business but thought it needed to recover to meet its minimum book-value goal. I asked Bob for a couple of weeks to put together an offer that would meet his goal. He was encouraging.

Three days later, I was in San Francisco in the office of Gary Rogers, CEO of Dreyer's, who had been our fiercest West Coast competitor when we bought Knudsen. He had sent me a gracious note after that deal, and over the years we'd become friends.

We quickly built a plan: I would buy Kraft's ice cream business and shift distribution to Dreyer's store-door delivery system. The plan generated an estimated $60 million in earnings before interest, taxes, depreciation, and amortization (EBITDA), valued at $360–$600 million, well above the $180 million in book value Bob was seeking.

By week's end, Bank of America approved a $250 million line of credit, co-signed by Dreyer's. I returned to Morrison with an offer: $190 million, $10 million above book value. He gave me a verbal green light.

Then came the curveball.

Philip Morris's lawyers objected to selling to a former employee without a formal valuation. An auction was scheduled for three weeks later. The short timeline meant few bidders could complete proper due diligence. It looked like we'd be the only serious contender—just like Knudsen.

Confident, I rented the upper level of the famed Four Seasons restaurant in Manhattan for a victory dinner with the Dairy Group team that had committed to return, and key Dreyer's executives.

The night before bids were due, a friend in Philip Morris's legal department called and left a message: *"Unilever is bidding. Their CEO wants to be the global leader in ice cream, and he wants Breyers at any price."*

My stomach sank. Unilever had deep banking ties, and they could certainly find out our ceiling and outbid us. I knew we needed to increase our line of credit, with assurances of confidentiality, to prevail.

I located Gary Rogers. We desperately tried to reach the CEO of Bank of America to increase our line, but he was out of the country. Nobody else we reached was able to make the decision. Apparently, it would have required the CEO to get the board of directors' approval.

Friday morning, we submitted a final bid of $250 million and were outbid by Unilever at $260 million, strongly suggesting they knew our limit. I made my disappointment clear to Bank of America.

The $12,000 Four Seasons dinner still happened, but it felt more like a wake than a celebration. I was crushed. Rebuilding the ice cream business would have been a challenge, but a very profitable one. I looked forward to working with Gary and the team, and I felt a sense of responsibility for the people who had committed to returning.

31

SPECIALTY FOODS AND EARTHGRAINS

IT WAS NOW JUST PAST LABOR DAY IN 1993. DURING THE SUMMER, I was approached to run a company formed by Robert Bass of Fort Worth, Texas, and a Dallas-based private equity firm led by Bobby Haas. They were very impressive, successful individuals who had acquired eight companies and were creating a holding company to manage them. They had acquired the businesses in February of that year, and the businesses had been operating independently since then.

Some of the appeal of the opportunity was to reunite the team that was ready to return to the ice cream business a few months ago. There was a whirlwind of activities between mid-October and Thanksgiving, and we opened our Deerfield, Illinois headquarters the Monday after Thanksgiving. Specialty Foods Corporation was officially born.

There had been little time for typical due diligence before accepting the CEO position. As a result, we moved quickly to visit all eight companies. Our new management group included Bob Baker, Larry Benjamin, and Mitch Weinick, who would be responsible for overseeing the businesses; David Weick (VP information systems), Jack Reisenberg (VP of HR), and Andrew Wyant (Rita's brother and our VP of strategy), who was joining us from the Boston Consulting Group.

By mid-December, the financial picture came into focus: we were $40 million short of the targets our investors had been told to expect.

That weekend, I flew to Texas to meet with Bass, Haas, and Doug Wheet, Bobby's partner. They were surprised and concerned, but unwilling to invest further capital. They suggested that our management team initially engage directly with our primary bank lenders, and that they would step in if needed.

Over the next month, I received a crash course in corporate finance. Bass's approach to acquisition funding was to offer banks above-market returns in exchange for substantial leverage, essentially paying higher interest for a smaller down payment.

The banks have minimum performance standards, known as covenants, and we had violated virtually all of them. There were penalties, of course, but after tough negotiations, we secured short-term relief. It was clear, however, that we had to significantly improve profitability in the coming year.

In 1994, we did exactly that.

Profits rose 80 percent over the previous year. By mid-year, we had a credible plan to meet our obligations to the banks.

We replaced or eliminated more than half of our business's management, and the new organizations performed well. There were significant cost savings in all the companies, improved marketing, the sale of two companies, and the acquisition of four businesses. In the process, we did lose three very competent leaders: Dean Metropoulos, who was running Stella Cheese, left disappointed that he did not get my job, which he probably deserved. He went on to purchase Hostess and became a billionaire. Sam Reed was overseeing Mother's Cookies and our restaurant business, Boudin's Café, and David Vermillion was CEO of Mother's Cookies. The two of them left and became chairman and CEO of TreeHouse Foods.

Most significant to me was that Mary Weinman Long, my longtime assistant at Kraft, joined me at Specialty Foods. Mary was truly outstanding—thoughtful, organized, and resourceful. She had spent over twenty years with Kraft and was an indispensable part of the Kraft Dairy and Frozen Division. She would play an instrumental role in managing Specialty Foods. More than that, she became a part of our family and a cherished presence during the next chapter of my journey.

Earthgrains: A Major Opportunity

The four years spent at Specialty Foods were high-pressure but exhilarating. The business improved to the point that we developed a plan to repay both the banks and the note holders and even provide a return to equity investors. The plan included continuing our successful acquisition program.

As we began planning for 1997, an acquisition opportunity arose that could dramatically accelerate our progress. Anheuser-Busch was spinning out its bakery, The Earthgrains Company. Earthgrains generated over $1 billion in annual revenues, about twice the size of our Metz Baking Company.

Our experience with Metz gave us confidence. Over four years, we had increased Metz's EBITDA from 3 percent to 11 percent. Andrew Wyant had relocated to Sioux City, Iowa, and played a major role in that success. He and the rest of our team were confident that we could apply the same strategies and generate similar improvements at Earthgrains.

But to buy the company, we'd need a significant infusion of additional capital from our equity owners.

I did not get an opportunity to present the case for Earthgrains to the equity holders. When I met with Bobby Haas, it was clear that they had already decided to stay pat. I was very disappointed. How could they make this decision without consulting the CEO?

Unbeknownst to me, a couple of key individuals within our organization had convinced Bobby and his team that Specialty Foods could continue delivering strong results *without* pursuing this acquisition and without additional investment. They also convinced them that they could manage the business if this led to my leaving the company. I told Bobby that I viewed it as a significant violation of trust not only by the Specialty Foods individuals but also by him personally and the other investors.

Bobby and I agreed that I would leave Specialty Foods. It was actually a very positive personal financial development. The company bought back my original investment at a profit, and they had no objection to my pursuit of the Earthgrains acquisition.

Within weeks of leaving Specialty Foods, I was able to find my co-investor for the attempt to buy Earthgrains. He was just down the road in downtown Chicago: Sam Zell, the legendary real estate mogul known for acquiring and turning around underperforming assets. Sam had a keen eye for value, and Earthgrains piqued his interest.

We attempted to buy the company directly from Anheuser-Busch before it went public. Unfortunately, they were firmly committed to the IPO path. So we crafted a new strategy: We would acquire 4.9 percent of the stock when it went public—staying just below the reporting threshold—and then we'd make a formal bid for the rest.

Sam Zell was a unique individual. He was of slight build but rode a huge Harley-Davidson. He rode worldwide, usually with a group of twenty to thirty. He invited me on a four-day ride in South Africa. I declined. We had work to do.

I opened a new office in Highland Park. Mary came with me—once again, my trusted right hand—and we brought in a highly recommended analyst, Andrea Brown. The three of us, along with Andrew Wyant, began a deep dive into the Earthgrains bakery business and planned on how we would run it.

We reached out to Earthgrains' leadership with an offer approximately 30 percent above their IPO and then-current price. They declined, stating that it would likely take nearly twice the current value for them to consider selling. We evaluated the possibility of a hostile takeover but concluded it would be prohibitively expensive and probably unwinnable, particularly after learning about a significant interest in the company by another large food company. It was ironic that we heard this from Sam's contacts at Bank of America. Rather than engage in a prolonged and costly pursuit, we sold our 4.9 percent stake at a small but tidy profit.

I was left sitting at my newly acquired desk, in my freshly leased Highland Park office, evaluating our next move. The Earthgrains deal had slipped through our fingers. While somewhat disappointed, I was energized to explore new opportunities.

It marked the start of a new chapter, the beginning of what would become a more than twenty-five-year entrepreneurial journey.

32

HERSKOVITS ENTERPRISES IS BORN

THE MORNING WE OFFICIALLY OPENED HERSKOVITS ENTERPRISES, the phones were quiet, new computers were not yet hooked up, letterheads, and just-delivered bank checks were on the floor. Carefully picked out artwork leaned against the wall, waiting to be hung.

It was a very different feeling from the years in the corporate world. No layers of bureaucracy, no divisions, no extensive people resources. Just possibility. Everything from here on would be ours—our money, our work, our decisions, and, hopefully, our rewards.

Herskovits Enterprises was our first choice for a name. While we considered elaborate requirements for investment, we decided on the following simple criteria:

- Invest in things purchased by consumers.

- Invest in situations where we can improve performance based on our experience and skills.

- Invest in competent people who have demonstrated the ability to create and run businesses.

- Invest only in people we like and would like to be associated with.

The logo was developed, and eventually, we created a website. We established banking relationships, and I funded our account. We hired an accounting firm mostly to handle our taxes and attorneys to handle the creation of the entity and future legal matters.

The "we" consisted of Mary, Andrew Wyant, Andrea Brown, Rita and me. Herskovits Enterprises was ready for business.

Hidden Beach Records

The Hidden Beach story actually began before Herskovits Enterprises was formed. In 1995, at a charity auction, we successfully bid on "An Evening with Ramsey Lewis."

Ramsey was one of the most accomplished jazz pianists of his time. His "In Crowd" recording had reached the top of both the jazz and popular charts.

Before the event, he visited our home to inspect the arrangements. He was impressed by our Mason & Hamlin piano, courtesy of our Dallas friend, though we had to have it tuned before his performance.

The concert was a revelation. In addition to his signature jazz numbers, Ramsey played several classical pieces, revealing that his career had actually begun as a classical pianist. Brilliant, engaging, and warm, Ramsey and his lovely wife Jan quickly became friends.

Given my business experience, Ramsey asked for my help with his finances. What I found was surprising and even shocking: he was *losing* money on many of his concerts. The breakdown was brutal—10 percent to his agent, 25–35 percent to the venue, 10–15 percent to Ticketron, 25 percent to the band, and 25–35 percent for transportation and setup. By the time everyone was paid, there was often nothing left for the star.

I knew I'd need help untangling this. Steve McKeever, the son of a friend, had created Motown Jazz and was raising funds to launch his own label. Steve, a Harvard MBA, knew the record industry inside and out. Within months, we reorganized Ramsey's entire operation, and in 1999, Ramsey had his best year ever.

I was very impressed with Steve—smart, organized, with a real instinct for talent and for music that resonated with audiences. We agreed that Herskovits Enterprises would invest in his new venture and help raise the remaining capital he needed.

Then Steve got a call that changed everything: Michael Jordan wanted to start a record label with him. Jordan loved the music Steve had produced at MoJazz and believed they could create something special. Raising the money became easy. There was no shortage of people eager to say they were Michael Jordan's partner, me included.

The business launched like a rocket. The opening celebration in Los Angeles attracted Oprah Winfrey, Denzel Washington, and countless other celebrities. Of course, following Rita's priorities, we were at a bar mitzvah in Long Island.

Hidden Beach Records became the only outside label distributed by SONY. Our first talent, Jill Scott, went platinum on her debut album—an almost unheard of feat for both a new artist and a new label. We received an offer from SONY to buy the company, but Michael and Steve did not want to sell.

Unfortunately, over time, the industry was changing. Increasingly, money was made in live performances, not record sales. Small record labels had difficulty surviving. Although Hidden Beach still operates today, we long ago wrote off our investment when label valuations collapsed.

Scorecard: 0 wins, 1 loss for Herskovits Enterprises.

JetFighter III

Mission Studios, creator of the *JetFighter* CD-ROM game (remember those?), was the first investment lead generated from our new website. They needed $250,000 to bring *JetFighter III* to market.

Mary, Rita, and I listened to the pitch but decided to pass as we had no experience with CD-ROM games. As the young founder was leaving, he casually mentioned something intriguing: he had the phone numbers of all 155,000 customers who had purchased and registered for *JetFighter II*.

That caught my attention. Over the weekend, Rita and I called more than 150 of them. We were shocked that over 80 percent knew *JetFighter III* was coming and were ready to place an order.

We called Mission Studios' founder back in and negotiated a deal that provided the $250,000 in exchange for 50 percent of the profits until our investment was repaid, and 20 percent thereafter.

Two months later, *JetFighter III* hit the market and sold out its initial run in just three days, fully returning our investment. Over time, the deal returned three times our initial outlay.

Scorecard: one win, one loss—but well ahead on the most important measure: total return on invested capital.

33

GOLF AND NATURAL GOLF

I WAS ON A FLIGHT FROM LOS ANGELES BACK TO CHICAGO AFTER a productive meeting with Steve McKeever at Hidden Beach. Sitting next to me was a gentleman wearing a Medinah Golf Club jacket. I had on my Winged Foot shirt, so naturally, the golf conversation was bound to start.

His name was Larry Olson. After a few minutes, he asked me to share the highlights of my golf experiences. That was an unusual request, but one I was happy to oblige. I described my initial lessons and my many trips to Scotland with my foursome of Buddy Stuart, Toby Walker, and Dick Dillon. I continued:

Kraft's World Series of Golf

One of the highlights of my "golf career" was the World Series of Golf Pro-Am in Orlando sponsored by Kraft. Our team included two U.S. pros, Payne Stewart and Jodie Mudd, the CEO of one of Kraft's top customers (an 8-handicap), a key buyer (a 14-handicap), and me (a 12-handicap).

The World Series of Golf wasn't a typical Pro-Am. It was a true competition among twenty-seven country teams, with major prize money for the pros and hundreds of spectators following every shot. The format was two best balls on each hole. With the crowds surrounding us, the pressure was very real.

The pros hit from the back tees—a bomb down the middle by Payne, a poor drive by Jodie. Our CEO guest was nervous and dribbled the ball about twenty yards. The buyer hit a low hook that struck a spectator about seventy-five yards from the tee. With the pressure on, I hit a nice drive down the middle. Payne birdied the hole, and I parred for a net birdie. This pattern continued. Payne shot a course record 62. I shot a 78, a net 66. Our team ended at -14 under par, four shots better than the runner-up South African team. Rita was leading the crowd with a "Go Lefty" chant because I am left-handed.

Payne became a friend, and his tragic passing years later in a private plane accident was deeply unsettling.

After the Phillip Morris acquisition, we fielded our own tournament. I got to play with Palmer, Nicklaus, and Player. Playing alongside the three greatest golfers in the world was surreal—a memory I'll always treasure.

Knudsen's Maui Golf Tournament

A couple of months after buying Knudsen, Sales Manager John Thompson invited me to their annual golf tournament in Kapalua, Maui. My reaction was immediate: *"Bankrupt companies do not often have golf tournaments in expensive resorts."* John agreed but pointed out that Byron Allenbaugh, CEO of Ralphs, had accepted an invitation. They were the largest and most important account on the West Coast.

I conferred with my boss, Mike Miles, and he thought I should go. I then conferred with my other boss, Rita, and she also thought I should go, along with her and the kids.

Kapalua was magical. The "Clambake" was three days of great golf on three spectacular courses, great food, nice people, at one of the most beautiful spots in the world. Our pro was Marty Keiter, the Bay course pro. Under his guidance, we played well and came in third out of eighteen teams.

From a business standpoint, the trip was an incredible success. We had been trying to get Breyers ice cream into Ralphs for over two years. Three days in paradise got Breyers into Ralphs. Based on this experience, we continued to participate in the Clambake for the next six years.

In our final year in the Clambake, I was no longer with Kraft and formed my own team. Marty was our Pro, and we were joined by my friend Toby Walker and a local friend, Rick "Bonz" Boudinus. It was the best team golf I had ever experienced. We had three hole-in-ones, Marty's 62 broke the course record, Toby (14 handicap) shot his first two rounds in the 70s, Bonz (4) averaged 67, and I (11) had three rounds in the 70s. We won the tournament by 13 shots.

Natural Golf

By the time I finished my golf stories, our flight was halfway to Chicago. Larry started. He owned Natural Golf. The Natural Golf swing was patterned after Moe Norman, a Canadian widely regarded as the best striker of the golf ball.

I gave it a try and was impressed. The swing was easier to execute and with less stress on my back. Larry sent a set of Natural Golf clubs to Florida. My first two Natural Golf rounds were in the 70s. I then had five friends participate in a two-day school taught by one of Natural Golf's best instructors, Todd Graves.

The opinions were unanimous. Natural Golf was an easier way to hit the golf ball. The company was undermarketed and generated only about $500,000 in revenue. I decided to buy the company. We made Larry a "fair" offer, and he accepted.

I recruited Andrew, Rita's brother, as CEO while I served as active chairman. Over the next few years, the company grew dramatically. We pioneered golf infomercials, recruited over three hundred instructors, and opened schools in virtually every major U.S. city. We signed six tour professionals, including former Masters champion Sandy Lyle, who saw dramatic improvement using the system. We even signed Moe Norman, and we generated widespread coverage of his unique genius.

Natural Golf led to some interesting experiences. Dr. David Nicholas called and said I had "changed his life." He saw me in the Natural Golf infomercial, committed to the method, and reduced his handicap from

15 to 10 while eliminating his back pain. David was the pastor of the 15,000-member Spanish River church in Boca Raton. He invited me to play with two of his parishioners, champion golfer Bernard Langer and Nico McBride, the drummer for the heavy metal band Iron Maiden. We had a great time.

Dr. Nicholas was brilliant. In Naperville, Illinois, in front of more than 20,000 people, without any notes, he gave a highly inspirational one-hour sermon. That night, we watched Nico beat the drums at the Aragon Ballroom in Chicago. It was quite a day for a Jew who usually listened to soft rock.

Another call came from the renowned motivational speaker and coach Tony Robbins. He also saw me in the infomercial, was in Boca for one of his dynamic presentations, and wanted to try Natural Golf. We set up a lesson at the Boca Rio Golf Club. The young lady in the pro shop froze at the sight of the 6'6" handsome and imposing figure. In about twenty minutes, our pro had Tony, a beginner golfer, hitting powerful 200-yard 6-irons down the middle of the range. Another Natural Golf success story.

In 2003, Natural Golf's revenue reached $20 million and was profitable. In early 2004, the company successfully went public on the American Stock Exchange. Based on an understanding with a large company to form a partnership after the IPO, we committed to our half of a twelve-episode Golf Channel prime-time slot. When the potential partner backed out, more than half of the money we raised in the IPO was effectively wasted.

At the same time, the Golf Channel raised rates significantly on infomercials, our best business-building tool. With many other commitments, we were forced to file for bankruptcy—a frustrating development given our prior success. We could, however, claim the most expensive private lessons and golf clubs in the industry.

Todd Graves eventually purchased the company's assets. He repositioned the company as the "Single Plane Swing." They have a smaller loyal following and have been consistently profitable.

34

IN-HOUSE TRAVEL AND SCOTTIE'S

HERSKOVITS ENTERPRISES' NEXT VENTURE SATISFIED OUR MOST important criterion: working with people we liked and wanted to be associated with. Frank Sampson and his wife, Michelle, were good friends. Michelle was, and still is, one of the funniest and most entertaining people we've ever known.

Frank was a seasoned travel-industry veteran with decades of experience across every facet of the business. He had an idea that I thought had significant potential.

It was the dawn of the internet revolution, and consumers and industries were just beginning to discover how to harness this new technology effectively.

In-House Travel

Frank's concept was simple but smart. In-house Travel would franchise travel agents based on either their location or their area of expertise. If you visited our website looking for a golf trip to Scotland, a boutique hotel in Rome, a scuba diving adventure in the Caribbean, or the best resort in Tahiti, you would be automatically connected to an agent with the knowledge and experience to meet your needs.

I agreed to serve as chairman and provided the initial funding.

At the time, the travel agent business was becoming increasingly challenging, and it was about to get even tougher with the emergence of new internet travel sites, such as Travelocity and Priceline. Inhouse Travel gave agents access to valuable incremental customers, often just enough to keep their doors open.

By the end of our first year, we had over 100 franchises, and the business was profitable. Less than two years after we started, we received an offer from Uniglobe, a Canadian travel company. With so much capital flooding into online travel sites, we knew it would be difficult to compete in the long run. We decided to sell, earning what I considered a reasonable return on our investment of time and money.

Now at two wins and two losses—a .500 batting average—I decided to stop keeping score and focus on growing our bank account.

Scottie's—A Familiar Concept Reimagined

Around this time, the internet bubble was boiling over. In 1997, Webvan launched with enormous fanfare, building automated warehouses to support its home grocery delivery service. They carried more items than a typical supermarket. It was a flawed concept, poorly executed. They burned through more than $1 billion before collapsing as the internet bubble burst in 2000.

By 2002, only one profitable home-delivery grocery business remained: a small operation in the Chicago suburbs called Scottie's. A couple of savvy bankers, Bill Steinmetz and Pat Pollard, and I purchased the company and guided it to profitability.

Scottie's offered a limited product assortment, anchored by a line of freshly prepared entrées. These refrigerated meals were high-quality food, reminiscent of the successful Village Deli entrées decades earlier. They quickly became the cornerstone of Scottie's business, accounting for nearly 20 percent of sales and driving profitability.

Scottie's success caught the attention of Nordstrom, which had invested in another home-delivery grocer, Streamline. They saw groceries as a way to expand their direct-to-consumer businesses.

Streamline was a public company that delivered groceries by installing coolers in customers' garages and placing orders directly inside. The model was novel but expensive. Streamline acquired Scottie's for $10 million, mostly in stock. Streamline's stock price doubled within a month, as investors assumed the business would adopt Scottie's profitable approach.

Unfortunately, they did the opposite. About six months later, they forced all their customers to install a cooler. We were stunned. How could they make such a move, and how could Nordstrom allow this? We failed to persuade them to reverse the decision.

Predictably, the business unraveled. Streamline filed for bankruptcy just three days before our one-year stock sale restriction was set to expire.

I was glad we gave up on the batting averages, as I'm not sure how we would have accounted for our success and, ultimately, our failure.

35

EVENT OF A LIFETIME—MY 50TH

USUALLY, A BIRTHDAY CELEBRATION WOULDN'T MAKE IT INTO someone's memoirs. But this wasn't an ordinary story.

It was late February 1997, just a month before my 50th birthday, and I was worried. Knowing Rita, I was sure that without my intervention, there would be an elaborate celebration. I am not a public person and dislike being the center of attention. A huge surprise party was not on my wish list. I even half-jokingly threatened divorce as a deterrent, though it was a hollow threat.

I kept a close watch for any sign of a surprise effort. I figured that if something were in the works, Mary would "spill the beans." Believing I was in the clear, I relaxed. We were headed to Las Vegas the week before my birthday, and I knew our good friend Lou Weisbach was hosting a dinner on March 27, the day before we returned to Highland Park.

The dinner at the Treasure Island Hotel was spectacular and included what I thought would be my only birthday cake.

The First Surprise

On my actual birthday, we had dinner reservations at a restaurant in downtown Highland Park. I overheard Mary: *"A table for four, with a birthday cake for Tom."* That sounded like my kind of low-key celebration.

Bob Baker, the menu, and me

Mary, my assistant, and me

When we arrived, David suddenly remembered he needed to pick up bagels for school the next day from Once Upon a Bagel. He asked me to come along to carry the order.

The shop was dark, the lights off, but the door was unlocked. As I walked inside, the lights blazed on, and one hundred and forty-eight people shouted, *"Surprise! Happy Birthday!"*

Everyone wore white T-shirts featuring a photo of me on a motorcycle and the inscription "50 More." Rita and Kathryn were waiting to greet me, though Rita quickly disclaimed responsibility. *"It's not my party,"* she smiled. *"The Perrauds did this."*

My resistance melted into enthusiasm. The party was fantastic—complete with a klezmer band, a magician/mentalist, and plenty of food and drinks. The celebration stretched past midnight. Somewhere along the way, cakes number two and three appeared, one from Once Upon and one from the restaurant where the cake order had not been cancelled.

I was grateful to the Perrauds for such a memorable night. Relieved that I had "survived" my 50th, I thought, Now we can all get on with our lives. What I didn't know was that this was the decoy. Yes, this major extravaganza was designed to keep me off track if I discovered anything about the real plan.

A Weekend in Florida... or So I Thought

The following weekend, we were headed to Florida. A limo picked us up and headed to O'Hare. As we pulled up, a well-dressed gentleman ran to the car and grabbed my golf clubs. He turned out to be the head of American Airlines at O'Hare, whose wife was part of the plan.

Inside the terminal, my eyes locked on a bagpiper playing in the corner, and then on a crowd of people behind him. They were my friends. Aha, I thought Rita had planned a surprise trip to Scotland, and these people are here to send us off.

I spotted Mary, my assistant, and asked, *"So, we're off to Scotland? And all these people are here to see us off? How nice of them."* She shook her head and whispered, *"They're all coming with you. And so am I."*

I quickly scanned the group. There were about fifty people, including our rabbi and his wife Peggy, close friends, and many business colleagues. *"Are they all paying their own way to Scotland?"* I asked incredulously.

Mary smirked. *"No, you are. Well, except for the rabbi and Peggy; David is paying for them out of his bar mitzvah money."*

Before I could fully process it, we were marching down the O'Hare concourse behind the bagpiper. This was pre-9/11, so no security checkpoints. At the end of the concourse, we gathered in a large party room for a two-hour send-off and my fourth birthday cake.

Then we boarded an American Airlines flight to London, in business class. Mary handed me the itinerary: two nights in London, fine dining, a theater show, a train to Skibo Castle for three nights, and then back to London before returning to the U.S. My brain instantly shifted into calculation mode: *I may need to take out a mortgage.*

We landed at Heathrow the next morning. Our family went to the Skibo Outpost, a charming bed-and-breakfast in Mayfair with all the amenities. The first event was lunch at a pub, sponsored by our good friends Staunten and Anne Flanders. That evening, our friends, the Levine's, rented out the entire famous Cecconi restaurant. Even though London is not known for its cuisine, we had fabulous food at both.

The next day, it was the show Martin Guerre, the hottest ticket in London's theater district. Then came the main event: Skibo Castle in northern Scotland. Transportation logistics were tricky, but with the help of our travel expert, Frank Sampson, everyone and everything made it, except for Rita's luggage.

The Marvelous Skibo Castle

Skibo Castle is located just west of Dornoch in the Highland County of Sutherland, Scotland. My first encounter with Skibo was when Toby Walker, part of our foursome playing at the nearby Royal Dornoch, wanted some cigars. We were told that the only place that may have them is the Castle down the road.

We entered Skibo's massive front door, and a distinguished-looking individual in Scottish garb welcomed us. The castle was breathtaking. It boasted 20 bedrooms and eight cottages. Our host excused himself and came back minutes later with four Cuban cigars. Toby whipped out four $100 bills, but the gentleman just shook his head and said this was on Skibo. I was very impressed.

Skibo was built in the early 1200s. For many centuries, it was the residence of the Bishops of Caithness.

Andrew Carnegie purchased Skibo in 1897 to celebrate the birth of his daughter Margaret. Carnegie spent over $2 million on renovations, turning it into a spectacular estate. Celebrities like Madonna and Michael Douglas chose it for their weddings.

About six months later, I returned with Rita. There is a tradition at Skibo that all guests dine together at Carnegie's massive dining table. On our first night, we joined seven other couples, and in an improbable sequence of coincidences, discovered connections with every single pair: two advertising executives, a Kraft recruiter, the son of a P&G VP, a McKinsey consultant, a Winged Foot Member, and even a Japanese businessman I knew from cereal joint venture talks. It was a remarkable evening of coincidences.

We joined the club the next day and made many trips to London and Dornoch. For my 50th, Rita and Mary rented the entire castle.

Arriving at the castle, the entire staff greeted us on the lawn. Rooms were assigned, and we settled in. Over the next three days, we celebrated and played. There was golf, tennis, falconry, off-roading in Range Rovers, swimming, and several other activities. I also enjoyed my fifth and sixth birthday cakes.

There were speeches galore, and I was humbled by all the kind words. The star of the first evening was Rita, who, luggage lost, appeared in her white "50 More" T-shirt, adorned only with her diamond necklace and earrings.

Jack, my brother-in-law, dug up fascinating history. Researching in the castle's reference library, he discovered that Andrew Carnegie's daughter Margaret was born exactly fifty years and twenty-eight minutes before me, on March 30, 1897. The staff believed Margaret's spirit still watched over guests.

Though I'm not much into the supernatural, the photographer who had taken over nine hundred pictures indicated that he could neither identify nor remove the squirrely lines in two of the pictures. One was taken when Jack asked for Margaret's help, waving a burning golf club cover from a brand competing with Natural Golf. In the other picture, I toasted Margaret and offered her a slice of my birthday cake. While I am no longer getting birthday cakes, I continue to toast Margaret twenty-eight minutes before the time of my birth on each March 30th—a strange custom, but one that reminds us of a truly remarkable event.

After three days, we returned to London and then to the U.S. Even twenty-five years later, people still talk about that trip. How Rita and Mary managed to orchestrate such an elaborate celebration without me suspecting remains beyond belief.

I would never have planned or approved such extravagance, yet it became one of the most memorable times of my life. The bonds formed among those who joined us will last forever.

It was an important lesson for me to "stop and smell the roses."

36

THE THEODOR HERZL AWARD

THE 50TH BIRTHDAY CELEBRATION HAD BEEN THE TRIP OF A lifetime. Just a couple of years later, in 2000, I was honored with another once-in-a-lifetime experience: receiving the **Theodor Herzl Award in Israel**. The award was presented by the city of Jerusalem.

Theodor Herzl is widely regarded as the father of modern political Zionism. Born in Budapest in 1860, Herzl moved to Paris in 1891. The antisemitic atmosphere he experienced there led him to believe that only by establishing a Jewish state could Jews bring about an end to antisemitism. In 1897, he convened the first Zionist Congress in Basel, Switzerland.

The award recognized my contributions to the Technion—Israel's leading science and technology university—particularly in food development and marketing, as well as for my work with Miles Lehrman in establishing the United States Holocaust Museum in Washington, D.C. The other honorees were Pennsylvania Governor (and future Homeland Security Secretary) Tom Ridge, Nevada Senator Harry Reid, designer Calvin Klein, and Russian businessman Mikhail Khodorkovsky.

Arrival in Israel

Rita, Kathryn, David, and I landed in Tel Aviv on a Sunday evening, August 20. From the airport, we were whisked directly to the historic King David Hotel in Jerusalem.

On Monday, we met Ehud Olmert, then Jerusalem's mayor, followed by Ehud Barak, Israel's prime minister. Both were engaging and spoke candidly about issues facing Israel. That evening, we dined with the award group. Kathryn sat next to Tom Ridge, and the two spoke for most of the evening. He was impressed and, by week's end, he offered her a job.

Masada and a Royal Lunch

Tuesday began with an unforgettable journey. We boarded Israeli military helicopters and flew to the ancient fortress of Masada. Kathryn and David were dropped off at the base and hiked up the steep incline. We were flown to the top. After a presentation on the history of Masada, we climbed into Jordanian helicopters and were flown to the palace of King Abdullah II of Jordan for lunch.

We were stunned. Here we were, an immigrant Jewish family from Highland Park, Illinois, dining in the palace of an Arab king. I hoped Andy and Béla could see this from above.

King Abdullah was charming and gracious. He had studied in the U.S., first at Deerfield Academy and later at Georgetown University. We recalled pleasant memories of Georgetown basketball, and he was amused that I guarded Dave Bing and Jim Boeheim in practice.

The conversation then turned serious. The King had just returned from a secret meeting with Hafez al-Assad, the leader of Syria. He told us that there was progress on a possible peace treaty involving Israel, Jordan, Egypt, Syria, and the Palestinians. Abdullah believed this was a historic step toward regional peace and prosperity. We were sworn to secrecy and overwhelmed to realize we were among the very few people in the world who knew of these developments.

Walking Through History: Petra

With a great sense of optimism, we got back into the helicopters and headed to one of the most remarkable places in the world. Walking through the Siq at Petra was like stepping back in time. The narrow canyon twisted and turned for nearly a mile, its towering sandstone walls closing in above us, before it suddenly opened to reveal one of the most extraordinary sights I had ever seen: the Treasury, carved directly into the rose-colored cliffs. The sheer scale and artistry were breathtaking.

It was hard to fathom how the Nabataeans, over two thousand years ago, had carved temples, tombs, and facades into the rock while engineering a sophisticated water system to sustain a thriving desert city. Petra had once been a vital hub of trade linking Arabia, Egypt, and the Mediterranean.

For me, Petra was more than an archaeological wonder. It was a testament to resilience and ingenuity—people creating something lasting against impossible odds. In its way, it echoed my own family's journey from Hungary to America.

That evening, we returned to Jerusalem. The kids collapsed into bed, but Rita and I stayed up late reflecting on one of the most extraordinary days of our lives.

The Theodor Herzl Award

Meeting Natan Sharansky

On Thursday, August 24, 2000, before being transported to the Knesset (Israel's parliament), we met with Natan Sharansky.

In the 1970's Sharansky emerged as the central figure in the Soviet "refusenik" movement. He co-founded the Moscow Helsinki group to monitor Soviet compliance with the 1975 Helsinki Accords. In 1978, he was charged with treason and spent nine years in prison. His case became a rallying cry for human rights advocates worldwide. Freed in 1986, he became a leading political voice in Israel.

Sharansky listened to our optimism but cautioned us. There were too many powerful forces invested in sabotaging peace, he warned.

The Ceremony—and Aftermath

The award ceremony itself was moving and dignified. It meant a great deal to me that members of my father's old friend Erno's family, along with my aunts and cousins, were able to attend. For a Hungarian-born Jew whose family had endured so much, standing in Jerusalem to receive the Herzl Award was profoundly meaningful.

Unfortunately, within weeks, Sharansky's warning proved prophetic. Ariel Sharon's visit to the Temple Mount, accompanied by hundreds of Israeli police, was seen by Palestinians as a provocative act. Rioting followed, escalating into the Second Intifada—and with it, the collapse of the peace hopes we had heard discussed just days before.

37

THE YEAR OF B2BILT, 9/11

BACK IN THE UNITED STATES, I WAS DISAPPOINTED THAT Sharansky's prophecy had come true, but I was focused on Herskovits Enterprises' next investment: B2BILT. The B2BILT story began with the build-out of the Specialty Foods headquarters. John McLinden delivered high-quality construction on budget and on time, a rare feat in the industry. I was particularly impressed with John and his attention to detail. After forming Herskovits Enterprises, we conducted a thorough study of the construction industry.

The construction industry ranked last among all industries in its use of technology to drive efficiency gains. Most construction profits were generated by mistakes, which were corrected through higher margin change orders. These "mistakes" stemmed from faulty architectural drawings, poor coordination among subcontractors, weather-related delays, material shortages, and other factors.

Founding B2BILT

In 2000, John and I founded B2BILT, a new company dedicated to developing technology that could significantly enhance the construction process. We had valuable input from professors and graduate students at MIT's School of Architecture, who were eager to advance construction technology.

The **B2BILT system** emphasized precision and communication:

- Rigorous focus on design and architectural drawings.

- Careful upfront planning to avoid errors stemming from poor coordination.

- Centralized control of material management, rather than leaving it to subcontractors.

- Sequenced construction activities with contractual accountability.

- Daily progress monitoring, with immediate remedial actions if needed.

Harvard's Design School took notice, publishing a case study titled *"A Study of Changes in Building Industry Processes."*

During the case study's formulation, the Fantasia Juice company was acquired by North Castle Partners, yielding a 100 percent return on investment for investors, including Herskovits Enterprises. The profit from Fantasia helped fund the final development of the B2BILT system. We were ready to expand. With two prestigious academic institutions backing us and real-world results in hand, we entered our first major investor presentation with optimism.

We scheduled the meeting for a Tuesday morning at our downtown Chicago office: six highly qualified investors, a morning presentation, and golf in the afternoon. We were confident that the story would resonate and that commitments would follow over a couple of post-golf beers.

The date was September 11, 2001.

The Shock of 9/11

The meeting began at 8:00 EST, starting with introductions, coffee, and small talk. Just before 9:00, Mary Danaher, our assistant, burst into the room: ***"Turn on the TV, a plane just crashed into a building in New York."***

In the next couple of minutes, we watched in horror as United Airlines flight 175 struck the south tower of the World Trade Center. And this was no accident, and there was no way to know exactly what was happening.

My first thought was of Kathryn, my daughter, who worked just three blocks from the towers. I dialed her number—No answer. At 9:59 am EST, the South Tower collapsed. We sat frozen, unable to process what we were seeing. Moments later, news broke that an American Airlines flight had crashed into the Pentagon. At 10:28, the North Tower fell.

Was this war with another nation? A terrorist attack. Were more planes coming? And where was Kathryn? Was she safe? Were *we* safe?

At 10:50, Rita called. Kathryn was safe. Relief washed over me. She had been walking to work and witnessed the second plane hit and the towers fall. She fled the area and later that day volunteered at a nearby hospital, using her language skills to translate for injured patients who didn't speak English.

By early afternoon, it became clear: Al-Qaeda, led by Osama bin Laden, had orchestrated the attacks. Nearly three thousand people died that day, thousands more were injured, and Lower Manhattan was left in ruins.

What transpired on 9/11 changed everything. It reshaped international relations, security policies, and daily life worldwide. It triggered two decades of war, beginning with Operation Enduring Freedom in Afghanistan. The costs—human, political, and financial—were staggering.

That morning, nine of us sat in our conference room, paralyzed, as we watched history unfold. We had come to discuss construction technology and investment opportunities. Instead, we confronted tragedy, uncertainty, and a world that would never be the same. Progress on B2BILT would have to wait. Like everyone else, we were left to ask: *How do we even begin to move forward after this?*

Streetscape

As we regrouped from the events of 9/11, our future path became clearer. B2BILT's system was humming, giving us a competitive edge over other construction companies. Developers recognized the value of our technology in delivering higher-quality construction more reliably and at lower cost. It also appeared that we could attract investors and build the organization. The B2BILT vision was to become a major player in the construction industry and compete for large projects throughout the U.S.

However, we could not escape a straightforward fact: The bulk of the profits on our projects went to the developers. Like many entrepreneurial companies, we decided to pivot as we learned.

STREETSCAPE was born.

The new company married a proven construction technology with an analytical system we created to evaluate development opportunities. We partnered with a young, aggressive, and competent realtor, Chris Feurer. Chris had a keen eye for development opportunities and identified the area surrounding Wrigley Field, home of the Chicago Cubs, as a focus.

Known as Wrigleyville, it was a lively area that attracted young professionals. Besides the iconic Wrigley Field, there were lots of restaurants, bars, and other places of entertainment. Wrigleyville also had several similar apartment complexes. Built in the early 1960s, it typically featured forty to fifty units surrounding a landscaped courtyard. These apartments were perfect for condo conversion.

Over the next five years, starting in 2002, we executed nine projects around the Wrigleyville area. The model was straightforward: we would purchase apartments for $60,000 per unit, and provide major upgrades, including new kitchens, bathrooms, flooring, HVAC systems, roofing, and other enhancements. The cost of these improvements was about $40,000 per unit. While we could complete construction in as little as four months, the process of removing occupants, finishing the work, and selling the unit averaged about one year. Approximately one-third of the apartment occupants purchased their apartments.

The average selling price was $140,000, resulting in a nearly 100 percent return on investment for Herskovits Enterprises. All nine projects delivered the targeted returns. During this "housing boom," we were helped by low interest rates and low down payments for buyers.

Location Changes

In the fall of 2002, Rita and I became "empty nesters" as David began his freshman year at Syracuse and Kathryn was building her career in New York. It was time for a change. We sold the Highland Park house and moved downtown to Chicago, closer to the Streetscape office. Rita was thrilled with our new home on the 57th floor of the Water Tower, where sweeping views of Lake Michigan and Lake Shore Drive created an entirely different rhythm to our daily lives.

A few days before David left the Water Tower for Syracuse at 6:00 AM, he corralled Rita and asked, "Guess who Gatsby [his Rottweiler] and I rode down the service elevator with?" He did not wait for an answer: "Oprah and her dog. She was concerned about her little puppy's safety, but once she saw how well Gatsby behaved, she was really, really nice. She lives right above us." We were big fans of Oprah, so this meeting was very exciting for all of us.

The chance to run into Oprah and the glamour of downtown Chicago were major positives of the move. Still, I found myself missing the familiar grounds of our golf club in Highland Park. In early 2003, we purchased a town home on Crofton South, adjacent to the 8th hole at Northmoor. We gutted it, and I redesigned every inch to match our vision. The design was admired and copied, suggesting that I might have become a reasonably good architect had I pursued that career. What would normally be a nine-to-twelve-month construction project was finished in just four months, one of the benefits of owning the construction company.

38

SYRACUSE 2003—A TEAM OF DESTINY

AS THE MODIFICATIONS OF THE CROFTON HOME WERE COMPLETED, Rita and I were glued to the television whenever Syracuse basketball aired. David attended the games, and if they were not televised, he would provide the play-by-play.

The 2003 Syracuse basketball season was magical. It came thirty-eight years after I first stepped onto the court at Manley Field House for my brief three-week college basketball career, and seventeen years after I slipped away from the Effie presentation only to watch Syracuse lose the 1987 national championship.

Like most seasons, I went in with hope, always believing Syracuse had a chance to win it all. This was Jim Boeheim's thirty-second year as head coach, and he had come close twice before. But entering the season, the team wasn't even ranked in the polls. On paper, this didn't look like one of his strongest squads.

Yet, I had a feeling. This was David's freshman year at Syracuse, and we shared a deep passion for Orange basketball. I had followed recruiting closely and knew we had a special freshman class. Joining the team was Carmelo Anthony, the nation's number two recruit behind only LeBron James, who went pro. He was smooth, confident, a natural scorer and rebounder who always seemed to rise in big moments. Alongside him came Gerry McNamara, a sharpshooter Syracuse had been recruiting since he was in ninth grade, and Billy Edelin, a talented guard who added depth. Returning was the athletic forward Hakim Warrick, whose length and energy gave Syracuse an edge inside.

Before the season began, I made a leap of faith: I put down a $1,500 deposit on a Final Four weekend suite at the Marriott in New Orleans, just blocks from the Superdome, site of the Final Four. Realistically, none of us thought Syracuse would get there—but at the very least, we figured it would make for a fun family vacation.

The Run to the Final Four

The regular season exceeded all expectations. Syracuse tied for the Big East title and finished 30–5, earning the No. 3 seed in the East Regional. They played brilliantly through the tournament, knocking off tough opponents to reach the Final Four.

The Herskovits family was ecstatic. We made plans to fly down to New Orleans early. Rita and Kathryn ultimately decided not to go, but David and I were all-in. By Thursday, we were checked into our Marriott suite—and thanks to David's friendships with Carmelo and a few other players, our room became a hangout for members of the team.

The semi-finals had us pitted against a strong Texas team. Given their relative proximity to New Orleans, it was practically a home game for them. The Texas game saw a magnificent performance by Carmelo. He had 33 points, 14 rebounds, and played strong defense, showcasing that he was the best player in the country and a superstar.

The final game on Monday night was against a very powerful Kansas team led by All-American Guard Kirk Hinrich. Gerry McNamara took over the first half, sinking six 3-pointers. Carmelo had his usual spectacular game with 20 points, 10 rebounds, and 7 assists.

The game was hard fought throughout. As the clock wound down, Syracuse was hanging on to a 2-point lead. With seconds to go, it bore

an eerie resemblance to the Heartbreak in New Orleans seventeen years earlier. The ball went to Kansas's Michael Lee in the corner, and he set up to fire a three-point shot. Hakeem Warwick flew across the court, reached up with his long arms, and blocked the shot. David and I were about ten feet from the point of contact, and the ball landed two seats to the left of David. The Syracuse fan threw the ball up in the air, and the celebration began.

A Memory for a Lifetime

The streets of New Orleans were filled with orange as the party spilled into Tuesday morning. David and I soaked in every moment. For four days, we lived in pure joy; a dream fulfilled after decades of near misses.

Over the years, David and I relived those nights in New Orleans many times. The 2003 championship was more than a basketball victory. It was another reminder of what it means to share moments with the people you love, to stop and smell the roses.

39

Whey Cool

D.J.'s Discovery

IN ADDITION TO BEING A GOOD BASKETBALL PLAYER AND A HUGE fan, David was a Junior Olympic rower. During the summer, he rowed for a club in Chicago, and I would sit on the hill overlooking the rowing canal and delight in the roughly fifteen seconds that I would see him and his boat go by. It was on this hill that I met D.J. Anderson, whose daughter was also a rower.

D.J. was a genius, one of the most knowledgeable people in the world of photography. He held consulting contracts with three of the largest photography companies. He became engrossed in nutrition when he was diagnosed with incurable testicular cancer that had spread throughout his body. He believed that a combination of nutrition and rigorous exercise could reverse his ailment. To his doctors' amazement, he did beat cancer and remained cancer-free the balance of his life.

Whey protein was a central component of his approach. Whey protein contains all the essential amino acids the human body needs, making it one of the most complete sources of protein available. Kraft was the leading producer of whey protein, a byproduct of cheesemaking. For years, Kraft research attempted to incorporate it into our products, particularly ice cream. Despite our efforts, we were unable to overcome its bitter aftertaste and ended up selling the protein to pig farmers for feed.

D.J. recognized that the proportion of essential amino acids in the commercially available whey protein did not precisely meet his body's needs. He balanced the proportions to the exact specifications dictated by the World Health Organization. This adjustment not only improved the whey's nutritional profile but also transformed its taste, eliminating the unpleasant aftertaste. After our kids completed their brief rowing triumphs, D.J. and I spoke at length about his protocol and his whey protein formulation.

The following week, D.J. handed me an ice cream pop that had 22 percent protein and was delicious. By mid-2003, we had developed a full line of products, including high-protein cereal, pancake mix, no-calorie syrup, smoothies, and more, all under the brand name Whey Cool. The products were protein-rich, packed with nutritious, natural ingredients, and lower in calories than competitors'.

Herskovits Enterprises invested in the startup, and we raised additional funds primarily from friends. A group from California with over one hundred weight-loss centers tested the products, yielding excellent results. Customers enjoyed them and experienced weight loss.

The weight-loss company claimed to have secured substantial funds for expansion, making a partnership attractive. Unfortunately, the investment funds never materialized. Despite the initial boost from our product line, the business, including Whey Cool, shut down about a year later. While I prefer not to delve into the messy details, the incident was unsettling.

Compounding my frustration was the thought of losing other people's money. This was on the heels of Natural Golf's failure as a public company, in which some friends invested. Although these events coincided with the bursting of the internet bubble, when the NASDAQ lost over 60 percent of its value, it offered little consolation. I felt responsible for the failure.

There was a positive relationship that developed through the Whey Cool experience. Jim Lavelle was a consultant to the weight-loss partnership. His Cincinnati clinic is renowned for creating holistic health approaches that improve patients' lives. Jim has a profound understanding of human health and has developed highly effective ways to identify and solve health-related issues. He has written over a dozen books on the subject. Before our West Coast misadventure, we created a program for doctors that provided a roadmap to help their patients. Our advisory board included some of the world's leading experts on nutrition and health. Unfortunately, the weight-loss company debacle prevented Metabolic Health Resources from ever launching the program. Today, Jim serves as the medical director of Lifetime Fitness, while his long-time, highly competent partner, Fritz Geer, manages the Cincinnati clinic. I still hope our concept can be resurrected in the future.

40

2003-2007 BOOM YEARS, THE PROJECTS THAT DID NOT HAPPEN

FOLLOWING THE DISAPPOINTING RESULTS OF OUR NATURAL Golf and Whey Cool investments, 2004 to 2007 were excellent years for Herskovits Enterprises. Our stock market investments more than doubled, and we had four outstanding development projects in Chicago. Fueled by low interest rates, minimal down payments, and relaxed credit rating requirements, we sold out all four condo conversion projects in record time.

While our real estate successes defined the period, we also evaluated other intriguing projects that ultimately did not happen:

- BevStar was an appliance created by an English engineer that dispensed carbonated and cold beverages like Pepsi or juice, as well as hot drinks such as coffee and tea, all from concentrate, all from one compact machine.

  The problem: the engineer could not deliver both hot and cold beverages from the same unit in the space on a kitchen counter under a cabinet. I lobbied for a simpler approach—one machine for cold, another for hot. But he was determined to pursue his all-in-one vision. We walked away. BevStar never made it to market. Meanwhile, the industry exploded with individual cold and hot beverage systems. With a different partner, our idea might have been a winner.

- With our experience at Natural Golf, we were among the first to be exposed to a concept called TopGolf—a high-end driving range that combined golf with food, alcohol, and entertainment. The economics worried us. Land acquisition and facility construction costs seemed too high, and we underestimated the concept's entertainment value. We passed. TopGolf went on to become a global phenomenon and was ultimately acquired by Callaway for $2 billion.

- A friend from my commercial production days at P&G introduced us to a TV production company seeking funding for a pilot of a new show called *Survivor*. The concept was compelling, and I was impressed by the producer. Still, television felt like an expensive, high-risk arena outside our expertise. We declined to invest. *Survivor* went on to become one of the most successful and longest-running reality TV shows in history.

- Perhaps the most unusual opportunity came through my friend Charles Everhardt. Together, we had the chance to help promote a highly anticipated super fight between undefeated champion Floyd Mayweather and his Filipino rival, Manny Pacquiao, to be staged in Dubai.

The Sheikh of Dubai had already deposited $180 million into escrow to fund the event. Herskovits Enterprises was negotiating a groundbreaking deal to broadcast the fight globally via pay-per-view on cell phones, with talks underway with major carriers across more than a dozen countries.

As a preliminary step, Pacquiao fought a warm-up bout in Las Vegas. The Sheikh flew in on his Boeing 757, and we were scheduled to fly back with him to Dubai to finalize details. The fight went twelve rounds, and by nearly all accounts, Pacquiao had clearly won. Yet, in a shocking two-to-one decision, the judges awarded the fight to his challenger. We concluded that a rival promoter had sabotaged the outcome.

With Pacquiao's defeat, the Dubai super-fight fell apart. Years later, Mayweather and Pacquiao finally did fight—but by then, interest had waned and we were long out of the picture.

Looking back, I've come to see that not every opportunity is meant to be seized. Some of the projects we passed on turned into billion-dollar successes, while others faded quickly into obscurity. The key was learning to balance vision with discipline—to recognize when to take a risk, and when to walk away. Those boom years taught me that success isn't measured only by the deals you do, but also by the ones you don't. We decided to focus on what we did best: building lasting value in real estate.

41

THE BLUFFS AND QUEENS TOWER

GIVEN OUR SUCCESS IN REAL ESTATE DEVELOPMENT AND THE challenges we faced in other ventures, it made sense to concentrate on real estate. The Chicago market had become very competitive, so we began looking elsewhere.

After ten years of living in Cincinnati, I believed the market was worth exploring. Cincinnati was not known as a "condominium market." High-profile failures during the 1990s discouraged developers from creating condos. In addition, the median price of a single-family home was among the lowest of any major metropolitan area in the U.S. Still, we believed that downtown development would create demand for affordable condominiums. Given our downtown focus, we named the Cincinnati-based company City Lights Development.

The Bluffs in Covington, Kentucky

The Bluffs met all of our acquisition requirements:

- **Unique selling point**: The property was located in the middle of a park overlooking the Ohio River, with a stunning view of downtown Cincinnati.

- **Affordability**: Units could be marketed to young professionals at prices comparable to renting.

- **Consistency with our model**: The project fit well with City Lights' development valuation approach.

We purchased the one hundred and sixty-unit Bluffs property in April 2005. Our plan called for four phases. The first fifty-six units were ready by November 1. With upgraded flooring, appliances, HVAC, bathrooms, and other features, they were an easy sell. On the very first day, I signed twenty-eight contracts. By year's end, the entire first phase was sold—the seventy-two units of phases two and three sold out by March. With prices rising rapidly, we decided to delay marketing the final thirty-two units until the summer. That decision proved costly.

Queens Tower

In March 2006, we acquired Queens Tower—a one hundred and nineteen-unit building perched on a hill west of downtown overlooking the city, where I had once lived while working at P&G. It was an excellent building, and the purchase metrics were even stronger than at the Bluffs. I provided the $2.5 million down payment.

Before construction was completed, we sold forty-eight units to investors. The plan called for all 119 units to be sold by the end of 2007. On paper, our Cincinnati projects would yield more than $10 million in net profit, enough to provide our family with financial flexibility and fund the charitable initiatives Rita and I envisioned.

The Downturn

By the time the Queens Tower conversion was complete, the economic environment had shifted dramatically. Demand and prices fell, and the last thirty-two Bluffs units sat unsold. Despite ramping up marketing for Queens Tower, we couldn't overcome the momentum of a deepening recession.

The crisis stemmed from interconnected forces:

1. **Housing bubble collapse**—Low interest rates and easy credit fueled a boom. By 2006, the bubble burst, home prices fell, and foreclosures surged.

2. **Subprime mortgages**—Risky loans were issued widely, bundled into securities, and sold with inflated ratings.

3. **Excessive leverage**—Banks borrowed heavily to buy these assets. When values collapsed, institutions like Lehman Brothers, Bear Stearns, and AIG teetered, spreading panic across financial markets.

With banks pulling back, mortgages were nearly impossible to obtain. In the first six months of 2007, we sold only three units. Our $10 million profit projection became a $6 million liability. Given my partner's limited resources, lenders, Bank of America and Fifth Third Bank, looked to me to cover the obligations.

Over the next year, I negotiated buyouts with both banks at about thirty cents on the dollar. As the economy worsened, both reneged on their agreements. To stay afloat, I borrowed $1 million from a small Chicago bank owned by our friend Walter Healy. Walter recognized the opportunity. He purchased our obligations from the banks at twenty-five cents on the dollar—less than I had offered. By early 2009, he had sold the remaining units from both properties, making a significant profit on his investment, even after forgiving the balance of my loan.

Reflection and Attitude

Resolving those obligations brought great relief. Unlike earlier years, I didn't "beat myself up" over the outcome. We had made sound decisions given what we knew. Few people foresaw the severity of the recession or its devastating impact on real estate development. I reminded myself of my stepfather Nathan's perspective during hard times: *"We still have more* *than the $7 we carried in our pockets when we stepped off the* US General Walker *many years ago."*

Through it all, I shielded my family from the worst of the storm. We sold our Crofton home and moved into the penthouse I designed and owned at Queens Tower. Kathryn became a partner in her NY agency, and David was in his final two years at Syracuse. Rita and I became Florida residents, enjoying winters at the Addison on the beach.

Although the recession had forced us to scale back and reset, I refused to view those years only through the lens of loss. We had endured difficult times before, and I believed we could do it again. What we needed was a fresh start and new ideas. As the dust from the financial crisis settled, I shifted my focus to other opportunities.

42

RECOVERY

THE HIGHLAND PARK OFFICES OF HERSKOVITS ENTERPRISES closed in 2007. After nearly twenty years of keeping everything organized and running smoothly, Mary retired to Anderson, South Carolina. There she met and married a wonderful guy, Dan Long. From that point forward, Herskovits Enterprises operated out of a small office at Queens Tower.

Around this time, my good friend Gary Greenberg—whose Sage company had been devastated by 9/11—was working with Feldman Advisors, a mid-market advisory firm founded by Howard Feldman. Howard, formerly the Managing Director, Investment Banking, at Wachovia Bank in Charlotte, had built a reputation for competence and integrity in the financial community. Over the next few years, I partnered with Gary and Howard on several buy-and-sell transactions, with a particular focus on food-related deals.

In addition to working with Howard and Gary, my main activities included trading public securities, serving on the Board of Liberty Tax, and resolving the final issue I had with Fifth Third Bank—the mortgage on my Queens Tower penthouse.

Successful Stock Market Investments

At the end of 2008, the NASDAQ had dropped to a five-year low, hovering around 1,600. The stock trading model I had developed when I first formed Herskovits Enterprises was flashing one clear message: *buy*. The economy was beginning to recover, and opportunities—particularly in the technology sector—were compelling.

I took out a mortgage on my Florida condominium and invested most of our remaining funds in the market. Between 2007 and 2013, the NASDAQ rose by roughly 150 percent. Our technology-heavy portfolio did even better, appreciating over 250 percent. The star performer was Apple. Guided in part by my son David, an avid Apple user, I accumulated shares at an average of $4.00 in 2009 and sold them at around $16.00 in 2012. That single decision was transformative for our financial recovery.

Liberty Tax and Franchise Group Inc. Board of Directors

Participating in the boards of public companies can be interesting and rewarding.

My brother-in-law, Len, introduced me to Ellen McDowell, whose brother, John Hewitt, had founded Liberty Tax. My background aligned well with the company's needs, and I accepted an invitation to join the Board.

Ellen, a highly respected attorney, proved to be an excellent board member. However, issues soon arose that led to John's departure as CEO. He sold his roughly stake in the company to a private equity group led by Brian Kahn and Andy Lawrence—two aggressive and highly capable former Harvard football players.

Brian and Andy quickly recognized the limitations of the tax preparation business—a conclusion I strongly agreed with. They renamed the company Franchise Group Inc., Brian became CEO, and the Board was reshaped with seasoned professionals. I was the only holdover.

Under their leadership, Franchise Group pursued acquisitions across multiple franchise sectors, growing revenue from about $150 million to over $3 billion. The stock price rose dramatically. Acquisitions such as

Vitamin Shoppe and American Freight were particularly successful during the COVID-19 pandemic.

As the pandemic waned, however, so did performance. The company was taken private—at a price I considered generous. Combined with the options and equity previously granted to board members, this transaction resulted in a very positive financial outcome for me personally. Unfortunately, the new ownership group faced challenges that ultimately drove the company into bankruptcy.

Settling with Fifth Third Bank

The settlement of my loan obligations to Fifth Third included the forgiveness of the roughly $250,000 balance on my penthouse mortgage. At the closing, a new manager reneged on this provision. With the assistance of my excellent lawyer, and now a very good friend, Robert Furr, we were able to resolve the obligation quickly. With this issue settled in 2013, Rita and I moved full-time to the Addison in Florida.

With our footing restored, I was eager to pursue the next opportunities that lay ahead. Two of those opportunities came to me in unlikely settings: a Cincinnati Reds baseball game and the Mirasol Country Club.

43

WINVIEW AND MARIDOSE

MY BROTHER-IN-LAW JACK INTRODUCED ME TO DAVE LOCKTON at a Cincinnati Reds game. Dave was in town raising money for his new company, WinView. Dave is a true serial entrepreneur whose ventures had already pioneered or expanded billion-dollar markets.

Dave was a Yale graduate with a law degree from the University of Virginia. Throughout his career, he has combined deep technical knowledge with an exceptional sense of emerging consumer trends.

Perhaps Dave's most outstanding achievement, however, was marrying Kathy, a brilliant marketer who had been the first brand manager for the Apple Macintosh. Kathy has been a major contributor to WinView's progress.

Between pitches at the ballpark, Dave explained WinView. The initial model focused on getting viewers to watch ads for incentives, utilizing WinView's synchronization technology.

I was intrigued. My own background was a natural fit. Despite its promise, we faced a significant hurdle: the high cost of customer acquisition. After careful consideration, we pivoted. In the European gaming market, roughly 60 percent of activity was in-game betting, requiring synchronization technology that WinView had pioneered.

Today, WinView's foundation of patents protects multiple business segments. We believe several major gaming operators are currently violating these patents, and we are in active litigation with FanDuel and DraftKings. As a result, I am unable to provide further details about the company's operations or strategy.

One final note: I granted shares of WinView to the original Whey Cool investors. Many of them have likely written off that investment by now, but I remain hopeful they will one day receive a surprisingly large return from WinView's future success.

Maridose

At the Mirasol Country Club in West Palm Beach, we were introduced by our friend Betsy Schneider to Richard Shea, who had recently launched a company called Maridose. Richard is a visionary entrepreneur who has succeeded in obtaining a rare U.S. government certificate permitting the sale of cannabis to researchers, particularly those developing pharmaceuticals.

I joined the Board and, over the past few years, have witnessed the company's growth into a promising business. The pending reclassification of cannabis will dramatically expand the potential market and position Maridose as a key player in pharmaceutical ingredient supply.

The irony of my involvement: I have never even tried a puff of cannabis. Yet here I am, helping build a business around it—another reminder that opportunity often appears in unexpected places.

44

Boca Grove, C1, InEnTec

When Rita and I moved full-time to the Addison on the beach in Florida, it marked our 21st year in that fabulous building. We were members of Boca Rio Golf Club, and the combination of beachfront living and a top-tier golf club gave us a truly enviable lifestyle. Still, there were drawbacks. The club was about twenty minutes from the beach, which made it inconvenient to pop over for a quick lunch, a casual dinner, or just a few holes of golf. Rita and I had decided that if the right circumstances ever arose, we would move to a golf community where all those conveniences were just a short walk or drive away.

That possibility materialized in 2015. I was playing golf at Boca Grove Country Club, just a mile from Boca Rio, as a guest of my friend Mike Fine. I enjoyed the course, but what really caught my attention was a striking building near the 16th hole: The Château. Rita and I agreed that we would only consider a condominium in a golf community. The Château looked like it could be the one. When I reviewed the floor plans of an available unit, I was impressed by the design, the generous space, enclosed garages, a twenty-four-hour concierge service, and other modern amenities. I told Rita, "We need to go see this place."

That same weekend, we hosted friends from Boca Rio at our Addison apartment. They loved it and, to my surprise, announced that they wanted to buy it. I protested, *"It's not for sale."* Their reply was simple: *"Everything is for sale."* Within thirty minutes, we shook hands, and the deal was closed. Suddenly, we needed a new place to live. The condominium at the Château was perfect. We bought it and moved in three weeks later.

We've now been living in Boca Grove for ten years, and we absolutely love it. The condo is spacious, beautifully designed, and surrounded by a community that feels like home. The golf course is excellent, the dining is first-rate, the new pool and gym complex is stunning, and best of all, the people are warm, engaging, and genuine.

Being at Boca Grove also opened the door to a couple of very interesting business opportunities—opportunities that once again reminded me that the right environment can shape both lifestyle and career.

Larry Dinken

At a Boca Grove Member/Member golf tournament, I was paired with Larry Dinkin. And about the 6th hole, we discovered a significant coincidence. We were both involved in the food business. He started and sold Marie Callender's to ConAgra for $140 million. He achieved this lofty valuation due to a bidding war with Kraft, led by none other than his current golf partner. This discovery led to an instant friendship.

Besides being a shrewd businessman, Larry is also an excellent golfer, tennis player, and renowned artist. His work is displayed in over thirty museums, as well as my apartment.

Condition One

Larry's summer home was in Long Island, and he was part of a group of business leaders who mentored budding entrepreneurs. There, he met an ex-Marine Sergeant, Matt DeMaio. While serving in Africa, Matt recognized that his men had no access to nutritious meal alternatives in the field. When he returned to the

States, with the help of a Marine nutritionist, he created a protein bar he called Condition 1, a term meaning "ready for action" in the military.

Matt is an outstanding individual. He has become a nutrition expert and has a solid understanding of the workings of the food industry. He is a natural leader and a pleasure to work with.

Condition 1 (C1) is sold directly to consumers through its website. It is baked to order and shipped fresh, differentiating it from the preservative-laden protein bars on grocery shelves.

C1 will generate over $1.2 million in revenue in 2025 with minimal marketing support. I have invested in the company and joined the C1 Board. We are developing several new products, including a cereal with the highest protein content per serving of any in the industry. Condition One Bars has also been selected for the U.S. Special Operations sports nutrition catalogue. This will provide direct access to 70,000 active duty personnel in elite units. I am very optimistic about C1's future.

InEnTec

Larry has a significant investment in InEnTec. It is built on MIT-developed technology that turns waste materials into valuable syngas. While others can accomplish this, the InEnTec technology is superior and patented. A major potential application of the technology is the ability to process plastics, turning them into valuable nitrogen gas without requiring sorting. It has the potential to significantly enhance the possibility of successful recycling.

I am an advisor and investor in the company. We are actively seeking a partner capable of building multiple plants to provide the necessary capacity across the country and potentially worldwide.

Looking back, Boca Grove has given Rita and me more than a beautiful place to live. It has been a source of friendships and activities that have kept us active and engaged. For me, "retirement" has never meant stepping away from work or ideas—it has meant creating a life where business, leisure, and community blend seamlessly. Boca Grove has become the ideal backdrop for that balance.

45

HEALTH CHALLENGES ADDRESSED, THE FINAL CHAPTER

WHILE MY BUSINESS VENTURES REMAINED STRONG AND MY DAYS were filled with purpose, the next chapter of my life would bring a different kind of test. After more than sixty years of good health, I began to face some significant physical challenges.

Fighting Parkinson's

In 2016, my good friend Dr. Steve Lipschultz noticed a slight tremor in my left hand. He recommended that I consult a neurologist. After a year of testing and observation, I was diagnosed with Parkinson's disease.

Parkinson's is a serious, progressive brain disorder caused by the loss of dopamine-producing cells. It can lead to tremors, stiffness, slowed movement, and balance problems. My initial reaction was fear. I had seen how the disease had profoundly affected the lives of a couple of friends, and I was troubled by the prospect of a steady, irreversible decline.

But I was determined to fight back. I quickly learned that Parkinson's affects people very differently, and that no single treatment plan works for everyone. With the help of my good friend D.J. Anderson—who had developed his own successful program to overcome cancer—we spent weeks researching the disease and exploring every possible treatment approach. While we knew a cure wasn't yet possible, we believed the symptoms could be controlled and minimized with the right strategy.

With input from Dr. Thomas Hammond of the Boca Raton Bluestein Neurological Center, we developed a comprehensive plan combining a nontraditional medication regimen with an intensive exercise program. I began working out regularly at the Florida Movement Center (FMC) in Boca Raton—a routine I've maintained faithfully for the past six years.

I want to express my sincere gratitude to the outstanding team at FMC for their expertise and encouragement—specifically, Michelle, who coordinates all the activities, and therapists Omar, Laurel, Courtney, Ashley, and many others who have been instrumental in helping me stay strong and steady.

As Parkinson's diagnoses have risen dramatically across the country, new resources and research have accelerated efforts to not only manage symptoms but also pursue potential cures. Approximately eighteen months ago, I began working with Dr. Richard Dewey, a neurologist deeply involved in cutting-edge research on Parkinson's disease. He currently leads a major study on a promising new drug and has been an exceptional partner in managing my treatment, adjusting medications carefully to minimize symptoms.

And of course, none of this program would be possible without Rita—my extraordinary wife and caregiver—who masterfully coordinates my complex medication schedule and keeps me on track, every day.

Thanks to these combined efforts, my symptoms from Parkinson's have remained mild, with only a limited impact on my daily life.

Back and Spine Issues

Unfortunately, in 2023, I began experiencing back pain that gradually worsened. What started as mild discomfort in my lower back evolved into severe pain radiating across my back and down my right leg. By early 2024, I could barely walk.

When my friend Dr. Lewis, a retired world-class surgeon, reviewed my X-rays and MRIs, he broke the difficult news: I had major spinal issues that would require a highly delicate and risky surgery. Because of the added complications of Parkinson's, he recommended I see Dr. Michael Wang, a renowned surgeon at the University of Miami Hospital.

Dr. Wang is meticulous in his analysis and accepts only cases he believes he can successfully treat. After reviewing my scans, he confirmed Dr. Lewis's findings. While the procedure would be complex and risky, he was confident that his specialized surgical techniques could yield a positive outcome. Normally, the wait for an operation was six to eight months, but in a stroke of luck, a cancellation opened up a slot later that same week.

I went in for the operation on Thursday, August 31st, 2024. Rita wheeled me in a wheelchair that morning. The operation was conducted on Friday morning. On Saturday afternoon, I walked without assistance out of the Miami Hospital to the nearby Brightline train station and rode home pain-free to Boca Raton—truly a miracle. I thank Dr. Wang every day for his brilliant efforts. I am continuing to recover and hopefully will be back on the golf course by the start of 2026.

In addition to Parkinson's and back surgery, I've also undergone cataract surgery, two root canals with crowns, a dental implant, and continue to manage high cholesterol.

Despite these challenges, I remain active in business, charitable work, and life. I am deeply grateful for the love and support of my wonderful wife and daughter, our extended family, and many close friends who make each day rich and meaningful.

I have had an excellent education, the opportunity to manage $3 billion-dollar companies, and have been involved in over a dozen entrepreneurial ventures. I have experienced religious freedom and have had innumerable exciting experiences. It has been challenging, engaging, and rewarding—everything that Andy, my biological father, Terry, my incredible mother, Nathan, my stepfather, and Béla, my life mentor, dreamed of.

It has been a long journey—from Budapest to Boca—and one I have thoroughly enjoyed. I hope that those who read these memoirs will find inspiration in my story and pursue a life as fulfilling as the one I have been blessed to live.

APPENDIX

1

KEY LEARNINGS

These lessons come from a lifetime of personal and business experiences. They are not intended as directives but rather as reflections and considerations for readers.

GENERAL LIFE LESSONS

- The most critical factor in a happy, fulfilling life is finding the right life partner. For forty-seven years, I've been blessed to share life with a wonderful woman. What began as physical attraction has grown into deep respect. Rita's warmth, empathy, and ability to connect with people continue to amaze and inspire me.

- Children can add tremendous meaning to your life. Watching Kathryn and David grow into capable, caring adults has been one of my greatest joys. Although my children were very different in almost every way, each gave us some of the most special moments of our lives.

- The passing of our dear son David from a heart attack at the age of thirty-eight has been challenging. Rita responded by establishing the David M. Herskovits Foundation. I have a difficult time facing up to the tragedy and try to prevent it from dominating my thinking. People have various approaches to dealing with grief. We need to identify and follow the strategies that will best help us cope.

- Determination and a positive attitude can overcome life's obstacles. When I was diagnosed with Parkinson's eight years ago, I decided to do everything I could to beat it. With the help of my doctors, I have been able to minimize the impact of this terrible disease on my life. While I am sure that medicine and exercise have played a significant role, I believe a positive attitude has been a major contributor.

- Be kind, but do not expect kindness in return—Dr. Lewis's motto.

IMMIGRANT LESSONS

- As a society, we need to be accepting of immigrants who seek to bring their ideas and talents to our country. It is widely recognized that America can provide the financial and intellectual resources to develop solutions to our most significant issues. Legal, controlled immigration has been an integral part of our economic development from the beginning of our democracy. While we need to deal with the problem of illegal immigration, we must ensure that "we do not throw out the baby with the bathwater."

- Many in the world are faced with difficult life situations. It makes sense for those to try to find greener pastures. Indeed, in my early years, my family focused on escaping tyranny to a country where achievement based on talent and determination was possible.

- It can take significant effort, resilience, and even courage to be successful in immigrating. Obstacles need to be identified, and methods need to be developed to overcome them.

- If possible, have representatives/relatives working to make it happen at your destination.

- Focus on learning the language as quickly as possible. Minimize communicating in your native language.

- Seek out government, community, and religious programs that can help you get established.

- Identify top-notch schools for your children. Be active with teachers and administrators.

- Organize all your essential official papers.

- Hire a competent lawyer to ensure all immigration requirements are adequately met.

GENERAL BUSINESS LESSONS

- Careful pre-planning and the anticipation of obstacles are often the difference between failure and success.

- Speak your mind. If people won't listen, they may not be worth your time.

- The ability to listen is a valuable skill. It needs to be developed.

- Before committing to ventures, assess the character and integrity of those involved. Today, artificial intelligence (AI) tools make this vetting easier than ever.

- Bravery, intelligence, and determination can overcome even entrenched challenges.

- Focus on a few priorities at a time, as it increases your chances of achieving them.

- Setbacks are inevitable. If your vision is clear, persistence matters more than perfection.

- Monitor outside forces closely; external events can shape outcomes as much as internal decisions.

- Favor decisions based on objective, thorough analysis over emotional impulses.

- When crafting strategies, think like your competitors to better anticipate their moves.

- Earn goodwill up and down the organization. Respect, warmth, and fairness go a long way.

- Adaptability is key—to markets, organizational changes, or unexpected setbacks.

- If there are five consecutive days that you do not feel like going to work, you are probably in the wrong job.

- Seek bold, decisive actions that can create step-change improvements.

EXECUTIVE LESSONS

- The first one hundred days of leadership are critical. Establish priorities and identify who will be responsible for executing them. Define your expectations of people and what they can expect from you. Detail your "likes and dislikes." Establish strong personal relationships with the influential people in your organization. Create "wins" to celebrate as early as possible. Meet everyone one-on-one.

- Managing a large team in a global Corporation demands different skills from building a startup from scratch, but both require vision, resilience, and empathy.

- An effective executive can identify significant opportunities to improve the businesses they are responsible for, even when those opportunities are not obvious. The equivalent of a basketball player who can manufacture his own shot.

- Reaching out to someone at the start of their career can have a lasting impact. Tom Laco and others did that for me.

- Being confident but humble enough to know who you can learn from and establish relationships, then make those people want to share their knowledge with you.

- Thinking and executing "out of the box" can produce superior results. Accept the inherent risk in deviating from expected or required behavior. Entrepreneurially oriented managers tend to advance more quickly than administrators.

- Find mentors you believe in and listen to them. But also trust your instincts when it matters.

- The brand management organizational structure works well in managing consumer perishables. Effectiveness is determined by the quality of the individuals in the system and the training that individuals have access to. Can work with either centralized or autonomous approaches.

ENTREPRENEUR LESSONS

- If you have entrepreneurial ambitions, write your ideas down. Outline them with simple steps, identify possible collaborators, and establish action steps to evaluate or execute them.

- Not every opportunity is meant to be seized. The key is learning to balance vision with discipline—to recognize when to take a risk, and when to walk away. Success isn't measured only by the deals you do, but also by the ones you don't.

- From my very first deal, I learned the value of making a fair offer. Over fifty+ deals later, this approach has consistently made transactions smoother, faster, and more efficient.

- Focus on areas where you have genuine expertise.

- When raising capital, seek investors who not only provide funding but also share your vision and can help execute it. Avoid those who don't align with your goals.

- Work with people you genuinely like and respect.

- Innovation thrives on the edges, often by those willing to cross boundaries between industries or between corporate and entrepreneurial worlds.

- The discipline and skill to execute effectively requires outstanding organizational skills, particularly in entrepreneurial ventures. If that's not in your toolbox, hire those who can help you.

2

FINAL THOUGHTS

WRITING THESE MEMOIRS HAS BEEN A LATE-IN-LIFE LABOR OF love. The process has reconnected me with memories both challenging and joyful. I have also been able to renew relationships with many friends and associates.

I have been fortunate to experience a broad spectrum of American business. Working my way up the corporate ladder was never my original plan, yet it became the foundation of the first twenty-five years of my career. The following twenty-five years were devoted to entrepreneurial ventures—an entirely different world. These two phases of my life brought dramatically different experiences and lessons.

As my time at Procter & Gamble demonstrated, successful corporations invest heavily in training and developing the skills their employees need to succeed. Along with exceptional, well-trained people, the companies I worked for also had substantial financial resources. That combination of talent and capital enabled the development and execution of ideas and the acquisition of assets to grow the business, as I was able to do with Knudsen and Frusen Glädjé at Kraft and with the four acquisitions at Specialty Foods.

Transitioning to Herskovits Enterprises, I managed my own time, had the flexibility to choose whom I wanted to interact with, and was able to be involved in businesses I could help improve. There has been significant financial upside. Jetfighter, InHouse Travel, Fantasia, and the dozen Chicago-based real estate development projects all produced excellent returns. However, financial risk is also a given—your own assets are on the line, and financial and human resources are often scarce. While our roughly fifty percent success rate is reasonable, it is still difficult to accept anything less than the consistent success I enjoyed in my corporate career.

Overall, I have had a fascinating mix of challenges and opportunities. I owe deep thanks to people like Dr. Wilemon and Tom Laco, who guided me early in my career, and to people like John McLinden, Andrew Wyant, and my assistant Mary, who accompanied me on my entrepreneurial ventures. Most of all, I am grateful to my father, Andy, and my mentor, Béla, whose dreams we were pursuing; and to my stepfather, Nathan, and my mother, Terry, who brought us to America, the land of opportunity we envisioned. And, of course, there is my wife Rita, who makes life worth living.

I wish I could end by celebrating America's greatness and the opportunities this country has given me, my family, and millions of immigrants. Yet, as I look at where we are as a country now, I am concerned. I am not a policy expert, and the objective of this book has been to tell my story rather than delve into the issues facing America. However, given my love of this country and the respect I have for the foundation created by our founding fathers, I feel compelled to comment... at least in this closing section.

It seems to me that we are not heading in the right direction.

Our politics appear to be the most significant cause of the issues. Too often, leaders in both parties ridicule one another instead of working together to solve problems. The justice system has been politicized and dragged into partisan conflict. Executive power is too often expanded beyond its intended limits, at times used to reward allies, punish opponents, or serve the personal interests of leaders and their families. Congress's approval rating remains at historic lows, reflecting widespread frustration with its inability to address pressing national issues.

Independent thinking is discouraged, and crossing party lines can spell political defeat. Public positions are frequently filled by loyalists rather than the most qualified candidates. Election results are shaped by gerrymandering and, at times, questionable practices. States and the federal government clash over responsibilities rather than working in tandem.

What we need is not more partisanship but more respect, cooperation, humility, and honesty. We need leaders who will listen and remember that public service is about the common good, not personal gain. Just as important, we need trusted, objective sources of information. Today, both political sides and their media allies too often trade in conspiracy theories, character assassinations, biased analyses, and outright lies.

Despite our significant challenges, I remain optimistic. My own life has been blessed with encounters with honest, ethical, caring, and exceptionally talented people. Out of the hundreds of colleagues, friends, and mentors mentioned throughout this book, only a handful fall short of those qualities. That gives me confidence. With the tremendous human resources this country has, we can overcome our problems and fulfill the promise I dreamed of as a boy, when I first passed the Statue of Liberty and gazed at the majesty of the New York skyline.

I am also very encouraged by the two young men, Abraham Flynn and Danilo Carmona, who have helped me with this project and with my other business ventures. Their technical knowledge has been invaluable.

The Florida Atlantic University high school program has provided an incredible education for these very talented individuals. Abraham has completed his first year at Northwestern University, and Danilo will be entering college with 3 years of credits. I am sure that they will make significant contributions to our society in the future.

I hope that the next generation of leaders will successfully address these issues and that the younger people mentioned in my memoirs can create and enjoy the American dream as much as I have over the last sixty-eight years.

Finally, I would appreciate any input from anyone who may have information that corrects or enhances the events I have described. There have been instances when I was unable to determine the exact dates or the sequence of events. If you have any corrections or additional input, I would appreciate it if you could let me know at herskovitst@gmail.com.

Issues Facing America

The following are not all the issues we face, but they are the ones I feel most concerned about.

- **The Deficit**. We spend beyond our means and pass the bill to our children. The last balanced budget was in 2001, and the deficit was $1.8 trillion in 2023.

- **Growth**. We need to continue to grow the economy to create jobs and help reduce the deficit. Over the last five years, GDP growth has averaged only 2.8 percent.

- **Inequality.** Too much wealth and power are concentrated at the top; The top 1 percent account for over 30 percent of the wealth in the United States, while average workers struggle to keep up. Inflation must be kept under control.

- **Health Care.** The United States is the only high-income country studied by the Commonwealth Fund that lacks universal coverage, and it ranks last among eleven peer nations in overall system performance.

- **Social Security**. The trust fund needs timely, bipartisan repair so people can count on what they have earned. It is expected to be depleted by 2033.

- **Immigration**. Newcomers have constantly renewed America. Forty-six percent of Fortune 500 companies were founded by refugees or the children of refugees. 71 percent of farm work-ers are foreign-born. We need a system that welcomes talent and treats workers humanely while securing our borders.

- **Climate and the Environment**. We must steward the land and air we will hand to our grandchildren. The year 2024 was the warmest year on record globally. Plastic, paper, and metal that could have been reused end up breaking down in landfills, releasing toxins and greenhouse gases. Only 4 percent of plas-tics are recycled, and plastic waste is creating major problems in oceans, rivers, and aquifers.

- **Education**. The United States is average or slightly above aver-age in math, science, and reading. Our students deserve the best in the world—stronger fundamentals, excellent teachers, and pathways to success.

- **America's Standing**. Favorable opinion of the United States is only slightly above 50 percent. Our credibility abroad rests on competent diplomacy, our fulfilment of commitments, and the example we set at home. We must stand firmly with our allies and keep a constant vigil on those who are not aligned with our democratic principles.

- **Diversity**. We have made real progress; now we must keep widening the circle of opportunity and avoid backsliding.

- **Infrastructure.** Roads, bridges, transit systems, water sys-tems, and the grid require sustained investment. The latest national report card from civil engineers graded U.S. infra-structure C- overall.

- **Public Health**. We should unite around vaccination, pre-paredness, and science to prevent the next crisis. In addition, we need to take full advantage of artificial intelligence to help cure chronic diseases.

- **Housing.** The current housing crisis in the United States is a deeply rooted affordability and supply problem: there simply aren't enough homes that people can afford. Roughly 75% of U.S. households cannot afford a median-priced new home. Part of the issue is the high cost of construction. The construction industry has made no progress in improving productivity over the last 50 years. Solutions to this issue are needed.

3

DAVID HERSKOVITS TRIBUTE

DAVID MICHAEL HERSKOVITS WAS BORN ON JULY 15TH, 1982. David was a precocious youngster with limitless energy. He began school in Gladwyne, Pennsylvania. The family moved to Highland Park, Illinois, in 1989. David attended Braeside Elementary School. He was very popular with friends and teachers.

David's first "big moment" came at his bar mitzvah. His sister, Kathryn, had done a brilliant job at her bat mitzvah four years prior, and David was determined to surpass her performance. He delivered his portion of the service in English, Hebrew, and American Sign Language. His performance was universally acknowledged as one of the best they had ever seen.

The following year, his first-grade teacher was diagnosed with incurable cancer. She asked David to deliver her eulogy on behalf of her students. He delivered a magnificent, heartfelt speech.

David was an exceptional athlete. He played football, baseball, lacrosse, hockey, and was a nationally ranked rower. He started high school at Brooks Academy in Andover, Massachusetts, and was on the varsity basketball and football teams as a freshman. He was a key member of the award-winning Brooks rowing team. At the start of his junior year, he transferred to Kent Academy in Connecticut, where he was the starting center and linebacker on the New England championship football team.

David followed his father to Syracuse University and graduated with a BS in business. David was passionate about the environment, particularly the development of alternative energy sources. He was a pioneer in the renewable energy sector. He held significant roles, including VP of international business development for Gigawatt Global in Jerusalem, founder and CEO of Energiya US, and VP at Brookfield Renewable.

Among his achievements was the development and construction of over $1.5 billion in solar energy projects. He was responsible for developing the first utility-scale solar farm in Louisiana. He oversaw major projects such as the sale of Otter Creek and Meherrin development sites, battery storage projects at Millinocket and Berlin, and the acquisition of the Goose Prairie.

David passed away in August 2021 from a sudden heart attack, despite appearing to be in excellent physical condition. He will be remembered as energetic, generous, and deeply committed to his colleagues and friends. He was a natural leader, determined to make a difference. He was known for his positive attitude and passion for life.

A Pictorial Tribute to David

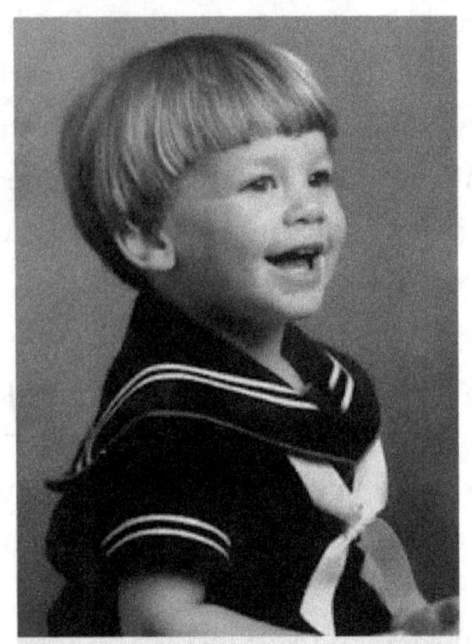

David at 2 years old

David with his favorite Wonton Soup

Even at a young age, ladies were attracted to David

A beautiful wedding

Perry Ellis's Sexiest Guy Next Door

THE DAVID M. HERSKOVITS FOUNDATION

THE DAVID M. HERSKOVITS FOUNDATION WAS ESTABLISHED TO honor the legacy of David, a pioneering leader in the global solar and renewable energy development fields. The Foundation continues its mission by expanding opportunities in renewable energy education, leadership development, and community-focused innovation:

- **Promoting Renewable Energy Education**
  Supporting programs and hands-on learning experiences that introduce students and educators to solar power, sustainable technologies, and climate change solutions.

- **Expand Mentorship and Leadership Development**
  Providing coaching, mentorship, and leadership training for both students and teachers.

- **Fund Scholarships and Grants in STEM**
  Offering financial support for students, teachers, and community organizations that advance STEM education, engineering innovation, and renewable energy initiatives.

- **Increase Access and Equity in STEM Opportunities**
  Supplying resources such as Solar Roller Kits, educator tools, and project-based learning materials to communities with limited exposure to scientific and technological fields.

- **Support Innovation Through Community Engagement**
Encouraging programs that incorporate creativity, teamwork, and renewable energy innovation, empowering students to contribute to a cleaner and more sustainable future.

The profits of this book will go to the Foundation to further their mission.

Visit the David M. Herskovits website for more information and to donate.

http://thedmhfoundation.org

4

OUR FABULOUS FEMALE FAMILY

AS I SHARED IN THE PREFACE, ONE OF THE PRIMARY MOTIVATIONS behind writing this book was to honor the family, friends, and colleagues who have helped shape my journey. Among them, a special group deserves recognition: the Fabulous Females of our family. We are immensely proud of all twenty-nine women and girls whose photos follow. While it would be impossible to capture all of their talents and achievements, here are some highlights.

The "Fabulous Female" family tale starts with the three matriarchs. My mother Terry's courage and determination are detailed in Chapter 1 and in her book *Once a Flower, Always a Flower*. She was a fantastic woman, loved by all. My mother-in-law, Margaret, was a sweet woman with a vibrant personality. Despite the challenges of being deaf, she raised four remarkable children.

Matriarch Peggy is a pioneer. She was the first female executive at Procter & Gamble (P&G) and, in her last position, worked directly for the CEO. She skillfully balanced a demanding career and the challenge of raising four precocious children. After leaving P&G, Peggy created a successful real estate firm. Her daughter, Missy, and her three daughters-in-law are all highly successful women who also manage careers and active families.

Peggy was my boss at P&G. While she had a very positive impact on my career, her greatest gift to me was personal—she was the one who persevered in getting Rita and me together. We met on a blind date, fell in love, and now, forty-seven years later, I cannot imagine life without her. Rita is a natural leader, respected, admired, and beloved by all who know her. She has built and nurtured relationships that bind our extended families.

My sister Judy has had a distinguished career. She was appointed a federal bankruptcy judge in New Jersey at a young age and later served as the state's chief bankruptcy judge. Judy is known not only for her brilliant legal mind but also for her warmth, empathy, and infectious smile. Her daughter, Dina, is an accomplished attorney focused on health-related issues and on her three talented children. My brother Mark's wife, Joan, raised two gifted daughters and was a highly competent and respected educator. The "Real Tom Herskovits's" wife, Andrea, is an accomplished retail store manager.

Our sister-in-law, Michelle, married to Rita's brother Kent, has been a serial entrepreneur since childhood. Today, she manages a spa and is an esthetician. She has three talented daughters and a son who just graduated from college. Rita's brother, Andrew, and his wife, Kelly, are raising three children; Kelly is a successful HR consultant.

As shown in the following exhibits, the next generation continues the legacy of excellence. Among them are a COO and partner of a major advertising company, the Editor of the *New York Times* Opinion section, entrepreneurs in real estate and public relations, a retail store manager, a model, a songwriter, and others. The younger generation is already showing signs that they will follow in the footsteps of the remarkable women who came before them. Watching their growth and development—and that of the precocious youngsters of the next generation—has been, and continues to be, a true joy.

"FANTASTIC FEMALE" FAMILY-- WYANT, SMIT

1st Female Exec P&G
Created Major Real
Estate Company

Peg Hogan Wyant

Spirited & Charming
Deaf Mother of 4

Margeret Facet Wyant

Real Estate
Developer CFO

Amelia J. Wyant

Opinion Page
Editor NY Times

Meetha A. Wyant

Leading SF
Real Estate Agent

Missy Wyant Smit

COO Civic Nation
Non-Profit

Lauren K. Wyant

Human Resource
Consultant

Kelly G. Wyant

Spa Manager
Aesthetician

Michelle B. Wyant

Songwriter
Performer

Emily Wyant

Model
Esthetician

Anna Wyant

Theatre Arts
Manager

Gigi Davis

Aspiring
Cross Country Star

Palmer Smit

Disaster Relief
Volunteer

Julia Wyant

World Cup
Skiing Hopeful

Finney Smit

Compassionate &
Artistic

Grace Wyant

"FANTASTIC FEMALE" FAMILY-- HERSKOVITS, WIZMUR, GLESER

Retail Store
Manager

Andrea Herskovits

Teacher Advocate &
DMH Foundation Director

Rita W. Herskovits

Holocaust survivor
Exceptional mother,
Wife

Terry G. Herskovits

Retired Chief Fed
Bankruptcy Judge

Judy H. Wizmur

Outstanding Homemaker
& Educator

Joan O. Herskovits

Chief Operating Officer
What If Media Group

Kathryn Herskovits

Speech Therapist
Presentation Pro

Rochelle M. Wizmur

Attorney - Health
Care Advocate

Dina G. Wizmur

Owner Public
Relation Firm

Arielle H. Silver

Teacher
Violinist

Jessica H. Szasz

Born 2016
Future Director

Ilana Wizmur

Born 2014
Talented Artist

Natalie Wizmur

Born 2011
Computer Gamer

Hadley Thompson

Director &
Determined

Maya Gleser

FAMILY PHOTOS

My Incredible Mother

Tom—Early Days

Tom—Executive

Tom—Entrepreneur

Tom and Rita—A 47-Year Love Affair

Meeting with Presidents

Meeting with Other Notables

A Passion for Golf

Major Family Events

Tom's Weeklong 50th Birthday Party

MY INCREDIBLE MOTHER

My mother and biological father Andy—married in 1946.

Terry and Nathan enjoying their 90s.

Terry joined her sister Shari in Rio in 1980.

Terry with my lovely wife Rita.

TOM IN THE EARLY DAYS

Chess with Béla and Kato.

Judy, Tom, and Tommy outside their apartment on the Danube River.

Tom and Judy

Fun with bike in Szombathely.

Teenage Tom, Judy, Mark

TOM AS AN EXECUTIVE

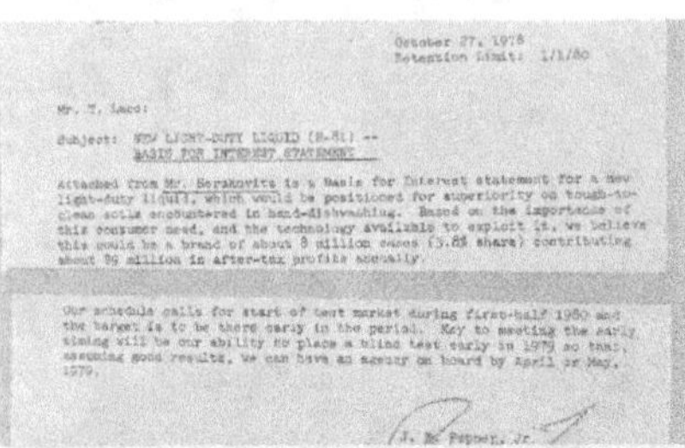

P&G memo to and from two of the
executives I most admired.

Tom—President of Kraft
Dairy Group.

An award from John Richman for
Outstanding Division Performance.

Tom—President of Breakfast
Division of General Foods.

President & CEO of $2
Billion Specialty Foods

TOM AS AN ENTREPRENEUR

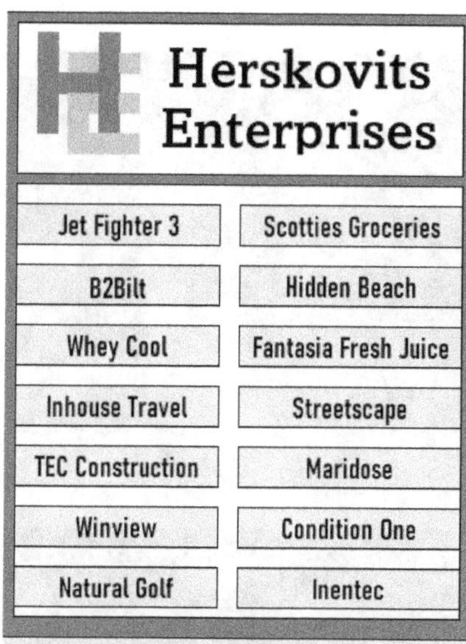

14 major Herskovits Enterprises projects.

Fun with Natural Golf.

B2BilT

A study of changes in building industry processes

Introduction

The B2BilT management team sits comfortably around the high table in the lounge area of their Chicago office, a large sunny, informal meeting area that is indicative of the B2BilT culture. Over a cup of coffee, they are quickly able to see the status of all their projects projected on three flat panel screens. A simple web interface reveals whether or not their customers are happy with a project's progress and the status of current issues, as well as cost, schedule, and safety updates for each project.

B2BilT has seen the inefficiencies and high fragmentation of the construction industry as an opportunity for change. Tom Herskovits and John McLinden founded B2BilT in 2000 to take a construction company to the next level by focusing on customer service. Through cultural change, supported by a technology platform, they have focused on being the project owner's advocate in the design and construction process. They view this as the means to change the inefficiency-laden building industry and deliver quality construction with major time and cost savings. To do this B2BilT has developed many technology tools to enhance communication and collaboration throughout the design and construction process. Having received a positive response from project owners and architects, B2BilT plans to continue to expand nationally, aiming to grow from a $25 million to a $1billion-plus company over the next five years.

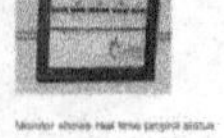

Research Associates Monica Lynn Tovar and Doctoral Candidates Katie Cacioca and Edrin Moralishna prepared this case under the supervision of Professor Spiro Pollalis as the basis for class discussion rather than to illustrate either effective or ineffective handling of an administrative situation.

Copyright © 2002 by the President and Fellows of Harvard College. To order copies, visit http://research.gsd.harvard.edu, call (617) 495-2041 or write to the Center for Design Informatics, Harvard Design School, Cambridge, MA 02138. No part of this publication may be reproduced, stored in a retrieval system, used in a spreadsheet, or transmitted in any form or by any means – electronic, mechanical, photocopying, recording, or otherwise – without the permission of Harvard Design School.

The authors acknowledge the assistance of: John McLinden, Tom Herskovits, Lori Brown, Chris Chapel, Kirk Gunderson, Marv Daneker, Dean Sanderson, Lieber Cooper Architects and Professor William Porter.

B2BILT—Harvard Case Study.

Natural Golf goes public; Andrew Wyant (Rita's brother) rings the bell.

TOM AND RITA – A 47-YEAR LOVE AFFAIR

Date #3 in Hawaii.

Enjoying a cocktail.

Wedding picture.

Enjoying a cocktail—a little later.

Le Santal, Saint Maartin—our favorite restaurant with the ocean behind us.

MEETING WITH PRESIDENTS

Tom is the Director of President Reagan's "Fun and Fitness" initiative sponsored by Post Cereals.

Time with George Bush at the Greenbriar.

MEETING WITH OTHER NOTABLES

Meeting with VP Al Gore at a private dinner.

Chicago get together with
Henry Kissinger.

A meeting with one of my heroes—
Senator John Glenn.

Kraft Dairy Group Headquarters opening
with Philadelphia Mayor Goode, Mike Miles
(Kraft CEO), and John Tucker (VP HR).

A Passion for Golf

Scotland trips: Tom, Buddy Stuart (6-time club champ at Winged Foot), Dick Dillon, Toby Walker.

World Cup of Golf—won tournament versus 26 international teams—Payne Stewart becomes a friend.

Annual Kapalua Tournament sponsored by Breyers Ice Cream.

A round with Arnold Palmer at Bay Hill.

Celebrating at our Winged Foot Club.

In a tournament with Don January.

Major Family Events

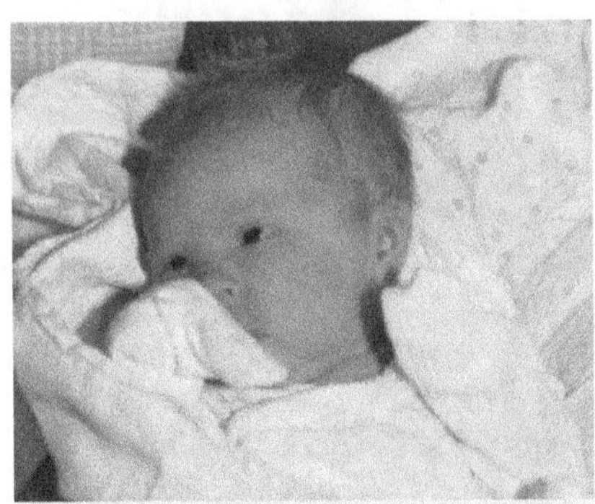

Kathryn is born—November 8th, 1978

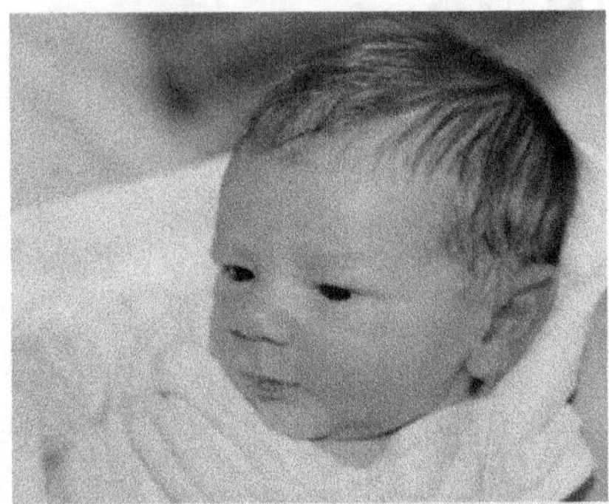

David is born—July 15th, 1982

Kathryn's Bat Mitzvah

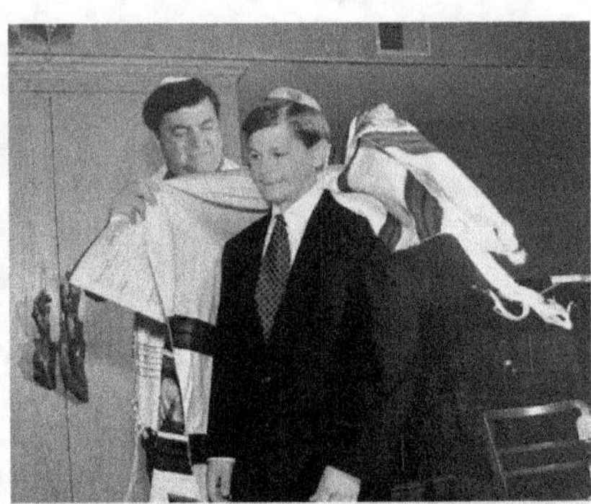

David's Bar Mitzvah

20th Anniversary at Kapalua, Hawaii

Tom's Weeklong 50th Birthday Party

Skibo Castle—Scotland

6

THE PS&D GOOD BOOK

A MEMO WRITING OUTLINE
B

C DATE	TITLE	AUTHOR	RECEIVER APPROVERS
NATIONAL PLANS			
D 05/08/79	ERA NATL. MARKETING AND SUPPOR	E.C. Strobel	R.R. Nicolosi
D 02/06/73	GAIN PAYOUT	T.G. Story	A.E. HARRIS
D 10/26/78	H-81 BASIS FOR INTEREST	T. Herskovits	J.C. SMALE
D			T. LACO
D			J.E. PEPPER
D			S.G. WEINER
D 11/12/79	H-81 NEXT STEPS TO TEST MARKET	J.N.Lilly/J. Mitchell	T. Herskovits
D 07/10/79	H-81-H-85 AGENCY APPOINTMENT	J.N.Lilly/J. Mitchell	T.Herskovits
PRODUCT TEST MARKET			M. Josoff
E 06/04/71	H - 34 BASIS FOR INTEREST	L.G. Ross	B.M. Moore
F 01/07/74	ERA NATIONAL EXPANSION	R.P. Hill	C.A. Lieppe
07/24/74	ERA WAVE 3 EXPANSION	T. Herskovits	C.A. Lieppe
F 06/20/77	CHEER W TEST MARKET RECO	J.D. Milby	F.R. Charron
05/25/78	JOY SUPPORT RECOMMENDATION	A.G. Lafley	N.P. Defeo
G 05/06/80	P&TPR TEST	C.M. Marhar	G.E. Lawton
G 04/25/78	ENJOY P&TPR SUMMARY	A.G. Lafley	N.P. Defeo
G 08/09/78	A DASH TRIAL PLAN	G.E. Lawton	D.I. Falk
H COST SAVINGS			
01/14/80	DISHWASHING COST SAVINGS	T. Herskovits	team of 30
I CALANDER YEAR ANALYSIS			
02/01/78	TIDE 1977 BUSINESS ANALYSIS	T.K. McCarter	R.R. Nicolosi
02/28/78	1977 LDL BUSINESS ANALYSIS	R.A. Cotcamp	D.L. Preuss
J COMPETITIVE ANALYSIS			
J 07/01/79	ERA,S RESPOSE TO WISK	R.A. Cotcamp	D.L. Preuss
J 03/14/74	WISK BUSINESS ANALYSIS	T. Herskovits	C.A. Lieppe
K RECALL			
08/18/78	IVORY SNOW RECALL	W.R. Impay	R.A. Bowles
L NBUS SUMMARY			
U & A SUMMARY			
04/01/74	ERA 12-MO U&A RESEARCH	T. Herskovits	C.A. Lieppe
M PRODUCT DEVELOPMNT			
05/01/78	JOY PRODUCT DEVELOPMENT	N.P .Defeo	
N MEDIA			
09/01/77	ERA SECOND HALF 77 - 78 MEDIA PLA	N.A. Cotcamp	D.L. Preuss
05/12/80	FEB-MARCH 1980 NIELSEN SHARES	J.E. PEPPER	M. Josoff

Note:there was no table of contents in the original "Good Book"

<u>GENERAL COPY FACT BOOK</u>

1. Value of Advertising
2. Advertising Philosophy
3. Advertising that Works
4. Copy Program
5. Evaluating Copy
6. Working with Agencies
7. Agencies
8.
9.
10. Copy Testing
11. Copy Terms
12. Introductory Copy
13. Copy Strategy
14. Brand Character
15. Creativity
16. Execution
17. Selling Idea
18. Slice of Life
19. Continuing Character
20. Testimonials
21. Commercial Length
22. Humor / music
23. Print
24. Demonstrations
25. Comparative/Competitive Advertising
26.
27.
28.
29.
30.
31.

7

ASSOCIATES & FRIENDS

THE FOLLOWING IS A LISTING OF ASSOCIATES AND FRIENDS WITH whom I have come into contact throughout my journey. The initial comprehensive list was over 300 entries. This required limiting the listing to more recent relationships and those that were particularly important in the past. My apologies to those whom I was not able to include. Also, due to the very large number of family members, they are not listed below but are likely mentioned in the text. An asterisk * indicates that the individual is deceased.

* * *

Abramowitz	Yosef	David's mentor, "Captain Sunshine" of Israel.
Ackerman	Ashley	Daughter of Billy and Debbie, mother of two, school teacher, a great gal.
Ackerman	Billy & Debbie	Cincinnati and Mirasol; Billy, a successful developer, and Debbie, Rita's golf partner.
Adelman	Shelly & Terry	Boca Rio members from Cleveland. Shelly is a successful businessman, member of Muirfield; owe him a round at Winged Foot.

Agran	Scott & Pam	Boca Rio members, the owner of Lang Realty. Great couple.
Anderson*	DJ	Developer of balanced whey protein, photography expert, exceptional researcher, nutrition expert.
Applebaum	Alan & Kerry	Past Boca Rio members, golf club champ, member of Cave Valley GC. Kerry, daughter of Joan and Kieth Jampolis*, my past golf partner.
Baker	Bob & Clarisa	P&G brand management, VP Ice Cream Kraft Dairy, VP Specialty Foods, VP of Strategy at Con Agra, executive recruiter, outstanding marketer, two very successful daughters.
Barnhorn	Brad	Founder of Fantasia, talented entrepreneur.
Belkowitz	Marty & Nancy	Boca Grove members, Nancy taught at Syracuse business school, Marty was an ophthalmologist and is a golf partner.
Benjamin	Larry	President Kraft Dairy and Frozen, CEO Stella Foods, CEO Specialty Foods, effective executive.
Berman	Jon & Barbara	Boca Grove members, Jon is a plastic surgeon, Barbara and I won the Sadie Hawkins golf tourney.
Bloom	Norman & Alice	Westchester, NYC, Norman was a cancer surgeon, and Alice was active in community affairs and had her own TV show.
Bleustein	Jeff & Brenda	Members of Boca Rio and Boca Grove. Jeff was a professor at Yale, moved to Milwaukee, and was CEO at Harley Davidson, credited with turning the company around; a lovely couple.

Boeheim	Jim	Basketball Coach at Syracuse 1976–2023.
Cardona	Amparo	Housekeeper in Philly, part of the family.
Carmona	Danilo	Outstanding assistant and computer consultant, very talented. Major contributor to this book.
Cohn	Bob & Sarah	Boca Rio member, often golf partners, both with single-digit handicaps, Sarah's mom was also a good friend.
Collins	Tricia	Assistant to Jack Wyant of Blue Chip Ventures.
Coslov	Michael & Debbie	Boca Rio members, the first investors in David's solar energy business. Debbie, canasta player.
Crane*	Allan & Lauri	Chicago, package supplier; chairman of Hebrew Seminary for the Deaf.
Dawson	Alfred & Amy	Charlotte, daughter of Levines. Both on the DMH Foundation Board.
DeMaio	Matt	CEO of Condition One Nutrition, talented ex-Marine.
Dewey	Dr. Richard	Neurologist, Parkinson's expert.
Dillon	Dick* & Phylis	Hispanic Ad company, golf partner at Winged Foot, and Scotland trips.
Dinkin	Larry	Investor in Condition One, InEnTec, creator of Marie Callender's frozen food line, sold to ConAgra, talented artist, good golfer, and tennis player.
Donatelli*	Miss	German Teacher, Clifton High School, English tutor.
Donovan	Steve	Era Brand Manager and Associate Ad Manager, P&G VP.

Dordelman	Bill	Executive VP General Foods, key contact, impressive executive.
Eckman	Melissa	David's good friend. A delightful person. Was a very accomplished accountant. Founder of Meli's Fit and Yogspiration.
Everhardt	Charles & Noreen	Entrepreneur, real estate, past client of B2Bilt Construction Company.
Falk*	Doug	Gain assistant brand manager, lived in Queens Tower, sidekick, passed away in 2024.
Feldman	Howard	Chicago, Owner of Feldman Associates, is a well-respected finance executive. Ex. head of lending at Wachovia.
Fergusson*	Charles	PS&D ad manager. Brilliant marketer. Passed away because of an unfortunate in-home accident.
Fergusson*	Jim	Chairman, General Foods, Ex P & G.
Feurer	Chris	Outstanding realtor, mentored David.
Fine	Mike & Narlene	Boca Grove members, golf partner, avid golfer, shoots his age, lovely wife.
Fiory	Nick* & Karen Schaefers	Owned a package design firm, New Year's Eve celebrant, wife Karen, one of the funniest people I know, very talented artist.
Flanders	Staunten* & Ann	Highland Park sponsored a pub lunch in London for TH's 50th.
Flynn	Abe	A sophomore at Northwestern, an outstanding young man, was our assistant in 2004 when he was at FAU High School.

Frank	Kascey (Robbins)	Married David Herskovits on March 2, 2019. A beautiful, intelligent young lady. An outstanding athlete in tennis and golf. Was a successful financial advisor for JPMorgan.
Furr	Robert & Sheila	Boca Grove members, Robert, an accomplished bankruptcy lawyer and mediator, Shiela, a psychologist and mediator, golf partners, and participants in FAU Lectures.
Garnsey*	Glen	TH partner, harness racing, Outstanding trainer and driver.
Geisler	Paul	First P&G boss, brand manager Bold, executive with Kimberly Clark.
Georgescu	Peter & Barbra	Ex-CEO of Young, Rubicam, similar refugee story, influential author and speaker on income inequality. A very impressive individual.
Goldberg	Richard & Mindy	Philly neighbor, Mindy, a SU grad in the SDT sorority, where I worked as a waiter, and Richard, a great guy, past owner of I Goldberg Army Navy Stores, now a realtor.
Goldhammer	Rabbi Doug* & Peggy Bagley	Spiritual leader of Bene Shalom.
Golub	Neil, Jane* Karen Gerhardt	Boca Rio member, Owner of Price Chopper, civic leader in the NY Capital Region, active philanthropist, excellent golfer
Goren	Ken & Marsha	High school neighbor, college roommate, and army bunkmate.
Graves	Todd	Natural Golf instructor, Single Plain owner.

Greenberg	Gary & Fern	Owner of Sage – TH Board Member, Managing Director of Feldman Advisors.
Greenberg	Rabbi Sol & Sue	Spiritual leader of Valley Temple, married Rita and me and David and Kascey.
Greenblatt	Kenny & Sandi	Addison residents, Tony-winning Broadway producers, animal advocates, and great people.
Hammond	Dr. Thomas	Neurologist, Parkinson's expert.
Hanlin	Dave	Las Vegas resident; ex CEO of Caesars Gaming, advisor to WinView.
Harris	Sheri	Highland Park neighbor, dear friend.
Healy	Walter	Banker executed Bluffs, QT deal.
Herman	Carol & Hank	Account executive at Grey Advertising, one of my favorite advertising people, very clever and creative. Owns an Ad Agency. Hank is an author. Three talented boys.
Honig*	Marvin	Creative director, DDB, created Gain, Frusen Glädjé ads, member Ad Hall of Fame.
Hopkins	Sheila	Gain brand assistant, Outstanding performer, Cheesborough Pond CMO.
Ivan	Doug	High school friend and fellow basketball player.
Jager*	Dirk	Worked on Gain as Assistant Brand Manager reporting to me; became P&G CEO.
Kahn	Brian	Major Shareholder of Franchise Group Inc., excellent CEO, very impressive individual.

Kaplan	Roger & Leenie	Highland Park. Son Scott Perraud David's best friend. Another son, Bryan, worked at Natural Golf. Responsible for TH's surprise 50th decoy party.
Kassie	David & Susan Harris	Boca Rio members. Canadians. David is the executive chairman of the largest Canadian investment Bank, Canaccord Genuity, brilliant, a great athlete (basketball, tennis), and a terrific guy. Susan is a highly respected consultant to the Board of Directors and a lovely person. They have two incredibly talented daughters.
Katz	Jorden & Barbara	Northmoor member; financial advisor.
Kilts	Jim & Sandy	Division Manager GF, President Kraft Canada, VP Kraft, CEO Gillette, partner CenterPoint, outstanding leader. Golf and fly fishing aficionado.
Kim	Don	Ice Cream Distributor in Hawaii for Kraft Dairy Group. Son Jason is a very bright food marketer, currently working with me to resurrect high protein cereal. Lived with us in Chicago while working at Natural Golf.
Kirstein	Harold & Gail	Boca Rio member. Owns a waste management business, David began his career with his company.
Klein	Scott	P&G Brand Management, Syracuse University graduate.
Korab	Bill	President Breakfast Food Division, First GF boss, instrumental in my GF career progress.

Laco*	Tom	Exec. V.P. P&G; Mentor and role model, instrumental in TH P&G employment, immigrant age 5.
LaValle	Jim	Partner in Metabolic Resources and Medical Director of Lifetime Fitness.
Levine	Leon* & Sandra	Founder of Family Dollar. Top philanthropist in Charlotte. Part-owner of the Panthers football team. Sandra is delightful. Visit the Panthers game once per year.
Lewis	Dr. Michael & Valarie	A highly respected orthopedic surgeon. Worked with Chicago Bulls and White Sox. Talented photographer and author. Inspiration for writing TH memoirs. Was voted best dancer at the Skokie Hospital Holiday party. Valerie is a brilliant intellectual who has been an active contributor to various non-profits, particularly focusing on the long-term health of our planet.
Lewis	Ramsey* & Jan	Chicago, a famous jazz pianist, TH restructured his company.
Lieppie	Chuck & Patty*	Worked with me on ERA; Initial intro dinner at the Maissonette.
Lipschultz	Steve & Leslie	Highland Park, doctor, Medical Advisor who detected Tom's Parkinson's and Rita's heart attack.
Lockton	Dave	CEO of WinView, bio in book.
Lockton	Kathy	Executive VP WinView, brand manager Apple.
Long	Mary Weinmann, Dan,	Exceptional assistant at Kraft, Specialty Foods, and Herskovits Enterprises, Part of our family.

Maggard	Karl	Louisville District Manager; TH sales trainer, reported to TH as brand manager.
Marcy	Chuck	Manager of Post Adult Cereals, President of Kraft Dairy.
McDowell	Ellen	Attorney, Board Member of Liberty Tax. Lovely person, very competent attorney, outstanding Board member.
McKever	Steve	CEO and Partner with TH at Hidden Beach Records.
McLinden	John	CEO B2Bilt, Partner in City Lights Development. Very competent construction manager.
Miles*	Mike	Kraft CEO, TH Boss at Kraft, Phillip Morris CEO, outstanding record of success, and attracted a very talented organization.
Moscow	Michael	VP Strategy Dart, Kraft, CEO Federal Reserve Bank of Chicago, is a very impressive individual.
Moskowitz	Rabbi	Yeshiva Eastern Parkway Hebrew teacher. TH tutor.
Moskowitz	Rabbi Phillip & Arielle	Spiritual leader of Boca synagogue; grandson of my cousin, a "rock star" rabbi.
Moss	Gerry & Eric Madson	Gerry worked with Tom at GF, Gerry Rita's golf partner, live in Naples and Portugal.
Neoporte*	Tom	Head Pro at Winged Foot Golf Club, TH instructor.
Nostrand	Kristen & Steve Junker	Kristen worked for P&G, a friend from the Lasantaville Golf Club in Cincinnati. Organizer of "girls of the gulf."

Pearlstein	Jim & Pam	Boca Grove member. Jim, past board member. Pam, canasta player.
Pepper	John	P&G CEO/Chairman; outstanding role model, excellent business judgment. Noted author.
Powers	Rick	Manager of Post Children's Cereals.
Reich	Woodgie & Carol	A Northmoor member purchased Crofton.
Reisenberg	Jack	VP of HR at Kraft Dairy Group, VP of HR Kraft Dairy and Frozen, VP HR Specialty Foods, valuable "right-hand man," very effective HR executive.
Richman*	John	Chairman at Dart, Kraft, a terrific person and outstanding leader.
Rodenstein	Howie & Susie	David's partner in Energiya USA.
Rodgers*	Gary	CEO Dreyer's, very impressive individual.
Salzman	Marty* & Allison	Highland Park golf partners, Lakeshore members.
Samson	Frank & Michelle	CEO InHouse Travel, experienced travel industry executive.
Schlau	Mark & Ratchel	Boca Rio members, good friends.
Schneider	Betsy	Mirasol. Introduced Richard Shain, Rita's golf partner.
Schneider	David	Leading Cincinnati optometrist. Golf partner, great guy.
Shain	Richard	Ex-P&G, Founder Maridose.
Sheriff	Fred	VP of Manufacturing, GF Food Division.
Simon	Marc & Marcy	Highland Park, CEO Halo, exceptional leader, great couple.

Skoler*	Lou	Extremely talented architect, Syracuse Professor.
Slavin	Arthur & Jane	Boca Rio member, Chicago, investor in WC, successful developer, very good tennis player and golfer, Michael and Peter's sons are great athletes. Peter was a good friend of David's.
Smith*	Phil	President, CEO, General Foods.
Smith*	Richie	Owner of Frusen Glädjé, friend.
Spear	Kathy	Legal Counsel Kraft Dairy and Frozen, excellent attorney, very strong interpersonal skills, and outstanding business judgment.
Steinhardt	Rabbi	Recently retired spiritual leader of Bene Torah, well respected, Inspirational leader and speaker.
Steir	Jeff	Kathryn's first boss; three-day stay at our house, 9/11–9/14/01
Stern	Carl & Holly Hayes*	Former CEO of Boston Consulting Group, vice chair of Goldman Sachs, and a most impressive individual. Holly was head of Strategic Planning at Kraft, a brilliant and very interesting lady.
Stewart	Buddy* & Karen	6-time Winged Foot Club champ, 6 Scotland trips.
Stewart*	Payne	TH Partner in winning the World Series of Golf.
Swartz	Jeff & Meryl	Boca Rio members; son works with Kathryn.
Szymanski	Susan	Flight Attendant at Capital with Rita. A dear friend.
Tannenbaum	Richard & Cindy	Golf partner and poker player, Cindy is an excellent golfer.

Tappan*	Jim	Executive VP General Foods, My direct report in the Breakfast Food Division.
Thaw	Maureen	Philadelphia Housekeeper, part of the family.
Tross	Ron	Bankruptcy attorney on Knudsen transaction at Sidley Austin LLP, a top-notch lawyer.
Tucker	John	VP HR Kraft Foods, Mike Miles's right-hand man, responsible for building Kraft's outstanding management group.
Turner	Welden	David's Boss in Israel.
Unknown	Margo	Hilda's friend, Rita's fan.
VanHorn	Jan & Kathy	Oxydol brand manager, now a member of Boca Grove, great guy.
Vismantis	Terry	Highland Park South Deer Park neighbor, Rita's golf partner, her home is a five-star destination.
Wade*	Gordon	A P&G legend worked together on WinView.
Walker	Tobi	California, 6 Scotland trips, Harvard MBA, real estate developer.
Weich	Dave	Information system manager, Kraft, Specialty Foods, effective manager.
Weiner	Sandy* & Judy, Ira	A very talented General Manager, a close friend and mentor, passed due to cancer.
Weisbach	Lou & Ruth	Creative entrepreneur, Halo founder.

Weiss	Morry & Judy	Moved into the Chateau in 2025. A delightful couple. He has been Chairman of the Cleaveland Clinic and Yeshiva University. Four sons. Varied business interests. Both Judy and Morry are brilliant, knowledgeable, and involved. Very philanthropic. It has been a joy to get to know them.
Weiss	Edna & Houni	Daughter of Erno Fleischer, my father Andy's best friend. A wonderful, caring person. Was "mother" to David when he was in Israel.
Wilemon	David B*	Marketing Professor, Syracuse, Advisor to TH and DMH. Highly influential in both of our lives.
Zell	Sam	Partner in an attempt to purchase Anheuser-Busch's Earthgrains.

GROUPS

Boca Grove Poker: Very enjoyable Tuesday evening game.

Participants: Stewert Kasen, Bill Turnoff, Larry Cohen, Richard Rosee, Howard Schnell, Alan Hutensky, Shelley Weiner, Marvin Gruber, and Mel Lazar.

P&G Brand Managers: *Dirk Yager, Neil DeFeo, Greg Lawton, Ross Love, Dick Nicolosi, Tom Newby, Dave Preuss, Rich Gold, Paul Charron, Pat Hill, Jim Milby, Eric Strobell, Paul Bressard, and others.*

GF BFD Talent: *Carl Harrington, Steve Burke, Karen King, Cynthia Velcamp, Laura McCorvey, Jane Drittel, Donna Webster, and many others.*

FL Movement Therapy Center: *Michelle, Omar, Laurel, Kortnee, Ashley, and many others.*

www.ingramcontent.com/pod-product-compliance
Lightning Source LLC
Chambersburg PA
CBHW051045050726
47592CB00002B/392